Fanny Crosby's Story

Fanny Crosby
(Frances Jane Crosby Van Alstyne)

Fanny Crosby's Story

S. Trevena Jackson

BAKER BOOK HOUSE
Grand Rapids, Michigan 49506

Reprinted 1981 by
Baker Book House Company
ISBN: 0-8010-5127-4

First published in 1915 by
Fleming H. Revell Company
under the title,
Fanny Crosby's Story of Ninety-four Years

PHOTOLITHOPRINTED BY CUSHING - MALLOY, INC.
ANN ARBOR, MICHIGAN, UNITED STATES OF AMERICA

To All Those

on earth and in Heaven, who have been blessed and helped by Fanny Crosby's sacred songs and joy-crowned life

There's music in the air
   When the infant morn is nigh,
And faint its blush is seen
   On the bright and laughing sky;
Many a harp's ecstatic sound
Comes with thrill of joy profound
While we list enchanted there
There is music in the air.

There's music in the air
   When the noontide's sultry beam
Reflects a golden light
   On the distant mountain stream;
When beneath some grateful shade
Sorrow's aching head is laid,
Sweetly to the spirit there
Comes the music in the air.

There's music in the air
   When the twilight's gentle sigh
Is lost on evening's breast
   As its pensive beauties die;
Then, O then, the loved ones gone
Wake the pure celestial song.
Angel voices greet us there
In the music in the air.

CONTENTS

Safe in the Arms of Jesus

Safe in the arms of Jesus,
  Safe on His gentle breast,
There by His love o'ershaded,
  Sweetly my soul shall rest.
Hark! 'tis the voice of angels,
  Borne in a song to me,
Over the fields of glory,
  Over the jasper sea.

  Safe in the arms of Jesus,
    Safe on His gentle breast,
  There by His love o'ershaded,
    Sweetly my soul shall rest.

Safe in the arms of Jesus,
  Safe from corroding care,
Safe from the world's temptations,
  Sin cannot harm me there.
Free from the blight of sorrow,
  Free from my doubts and fears:
Only a few more trials,
  Only a few more tears!

Jesus, my heart's dear refuge,
  Jesus has died for me:
Firm on the Rock of Ages
  Ever my trust shall be.
Here let me wait with patience,
  Wait till the night is o'er:
Wait till I see the morning
  Break on the golden shore.

[*1868*]

ILLUSTRATIONS

In the year 1872, Frances Ridley Havergal, one of England's sweetest sacred singers and saintliest women, paid the following beautiful tribute to Fanny Crosby, her sister hymn-writer in America.

Sweet blind singer over the sea,
Tuneful and jubilant! how can it be
That the songs of gladness, which float so far,
As if they fell from the evening star,
Are the notes of one who may never see
"Visible music" of flower and tree,
Purple of mountain, or glitter of snow,
Ruby and gold of the sunset glow,
And never the light of a loving face?
Must not the world be a desolate place
For eyes that are sealed with the seal of years,
Eyes that are open only for tears?
How can she sing in the dark like this?
What is her fountain of light and bliss?

O, her heart can see, her heart can see!
And its sight is strong and swift and free;
Never the ken of mortal eye
Could pierce so deep and far and high
As the eagle vision of hearts that dwell
In the lofty, sunlit citadel
Of Faith that overcomes the world,
With banners of Hope and Joy unfurled,
Garrisoned with God's perfect peace,
Ringing with pæans that never cease,
Flooded with splendour bright and broad,
The glorious light of the Love of God.

Her heart can see, her heart can see!
Well may she sing so joyously!
For the King Himself, in His tender grace
Hath shown her the brightness of His face;
And who shall pine for a glow-worm light
When the sun goes forth in His radiant might?
She can read His law, as a shining chart,
For His finger hath written it on her heart;
She can read His love, for on all her way
His hand is writing it every day.
"Bright cloud" indeed must that darkness be,
When "Jesus only" the heart can see.

* * * * *

Dear blind sister over the sea
An English heart goes forth to thee.
We are linked by a cable of faith and song
Flashing bright sympathy swift along;
One in the East and one in the West
Singing for Him whom our souls love best,
"Singing for Jesus," telling His love
All the way to our home above,
Where the severing sea, with its restless tide,
Never shall hinder and never divide.
Sister! what shall our meeting be,
When our hearts shall sing, and our eyes shall see!

Lincoln the Great

I

With loyal devotion again we recall
The birthday of Lincoln so dear to us all;
Our president, hero, and statesman in one,
As firm as a rock and as true as the sun;
An honest defender of justice and truth,
A brilliant example he leaves for our youth,
The words he has spoken, the deeds he has wrought,
A lesson of wisdom and patience have taught.

II

When wildly the ship of our union was tossed,
And sages predicted that all would be lost,
Still, still at the helm like a giant he stood,
With courage undaunted repelling the flood.
Then lifting his eyes from the storm-girded wave,
And looking to Jesus the mighty to save,
Though billows were raging and thunders were loud,
He saw like a vision God's bow in the cloud.

III

His strong resolution no mortal could shake,
The old Constitution he would not forsake,
He reverenced his country and honored its laws,
A martyr to freedom he died in her cause.
The pages of history, the annals of fame,
The voice of the nation his greatness proclaim,
The world like a trumpet reechoes his worth,
And crowns with bright laurels the day of his birth.

[*February, 1909*] FANNY J. CROSBY.

I

"Aunt Fanny"

Trustfully, trustfully
  Come I to Thee;
Jesus, Thou blessed One,
  Thine would I be;
Then shall I cheerfully,
  Truly and earnestly
Walk in Thy Spirit,
  Saviour, with Thee.

Peacefully, peacefully
  Come I to Thee;
More of Thy presence, Lord,
  Grant Thou to me;
Then shall I carefully,
  Watchfully, prayerfully
Walk in Thy Spirit,
  Closer to Thee.

Joyfully, joyfully
  Come I to Thee;
Thou art my loving Friend,
  Precious to me;
O may I restfully,
  Calmly and lovingly
Dwell in Thy Spirit,
  Saviour, with Thee.

I

"AUNT FANNY"

"Singing for Jesus, telling His love
All the way to the home above,
Where the severing sea with its restless tide
Never shall hinder, and never divide."

THIS little book has been written in loving appreciation of one whom I knew intimately for many years, and whose hymns I have sung since baby-days. No attempt has been made to present a critical study of Frances Jane Crosby, but simply to retell the life of the Sightless Singer as she, herself, told it to me on various occasions when visiting my home. What has been brought together will, I trust, prove both pleasurable and profitable to men and women everywhere, who have been helped and blessed by her ministry of sacred song.

I met Fanny Crosby before I went to college, and I made up my mind that when I became a minister of the Gospel and living in a manse, the first notable person I would entertain should be Fanny Crosby. It is now twenty years ago since our home was first honoured with her presence, and each year down to 1914 she was an annual guest. During these years I noted five outstanding characteristics in her life.

First, her diligent industry. Aunt Fanny was one of the most industrious souls I have ever known. Whenever she came to visit us her little work-bag and knitting needles were ever present. She delighted in knitting wash-rags for her friends. It seemed quite impossible for her to be idle. Some one must be reading to her, or she must be working out some poem, or plying her needle, or what not. Aunt Fanny was the soul of industry.

Then there was her wonderful memory.

It was in every way remarkable. In relating her story to me she was always able to recall her poems at will, and quote them without missing a word. In the church services she would sing her own hymns with the choir and congregation with as much ease and accuracy as those who had the books in their hands, and in place of reading a set lesson from the Scriptures, would repeat chapters from the Bible.

Again, an outstanding unselfishness possessed her through all the days of her life. She could have been a rich woman had she cared to become one; but she poured out the wealth of her heart and mind solely to make others happier and better. Often when a donation was presented to her from an individual or the church, she would protest that she was being given too much; and she often shared what she received with those who needed it more than herself.

Then there was her unfailing joyousness, which was as a sunbeam wherever she went. I never once heard her utter a sad or regretful note. She was at all times as lively as a cricket. There was always a bright light in her cloud. One of her favourite expressions was: "Bless your dear soul, I am so happy to *see* you." This spirit of joy she scattered everywhere she went, among old and young, rich and poor. To feel glum or depressed with Aunt Fanny around so full of real joyousness brought always a sense of reproach. Her joy was infectious. People caught its spirit and gathered it into their own hearts.

Finally, there was her wonderful, unfailing sympathy. In my intimate acquaintance with Fanny Crosby for over twenty years, I must confess that I have not found a person with so many cupfuls of comfort for burdened and distressed souls. Hundreds of her hymns were nothing more than the outpouring of her cup of comfort to make the weak strong, and the blind to see. If she knew of a troubled heart or a wounded body among her friends, it mattered not how far away the sufferer might be, Fanny could not retire at night until she had thought out of her heart some message for the troubled soul.

While visiting our home about three years ago, she heard of one of her blind school friends, by the name of Alice Holmes, whom she had not seen in forty years. Alice was sick and Fanny said, "Dear Alice, I am two years older than she. We roomed together in the Institution for the Blind. I wish I could see and help her." The next day a friend took Fanny to see her suffering schoolmate, and I accompanied her. Alice Holmes was somewhat deaf, but she knew the voice of her school chum of seventy-five years before. Aunt Fanny placed her arms around Alice's neck and kissed and hugged her, and the two blind women wept. I sat in silence as Fanny poured out the sympathy of her heart and cheered her stricken friend. As we came away Alice said, "Fan, you have greatly helped me to-day, and my soul is comforted by your visit. I have long desired to see you. Good-bye, Fan; we shall meet again in the better land."

Fanny Crosby not only sought to strengthen the hearts of individuals but she sent constantly her cup of comfort to the church as well. It was my custom, once a year, to send her a birthday present. On her ninetieth birthday I sent her one hundred beautiful carnations and she sent this message in return:

> Dear friends, my heart is with you,
> Your kindness I recall;
> And on my ninetieth birthday
> I greet you one and all.

Oh, glory be to Jesus,
My Saviour, friend, and guide;
I'm going home to praise Him,
I'm walking by His side.
God keep thee, faithful pastor,
And shield thee from above,
Beneath His royal banner,
Of mercy, peace, and love.

When Mr. Sankey lay sick and nigh unto death Fanny could not rest at home in Bridgeport. She must go to him and give him the comfort of her own heart. She took to him a chalice full of consolation, and wonderfully helped the great gospel singer in the struggle through which he passed in the last days of his earthly pilgrimage. The two sightless servants of God (Mr. Sankey was blind for some years) sat together and talked of days gone by. Then God's Holy Book was read, prayer offered, one of their old battle hymns sung, and Fanny went away. But Sankey felt that an angel-hand of strength had been held out to him, and that the presence of Fanny Crosby had been to his heart as a healing balm.

On one occasion I took her to a family that had undergone a great struggle, where the darkness was so thick that it could almost be felt. Poverty's hand had suddenly reached the home, for death had recently taken the father and bread-winner to the land of spirits. There seemed to be none capable of comforting these people who had seen better and brighter days. But when Fanny entered, she was as skillful in her use of words as an angel spirit. She talked as one inspired of God. Then she prayed, and what a prayer of comfort it was! Before leaving she gave to the stricken family a part of the money the church had given to her and said, "I want you to remember Jehovah-Jireth. It means 'The Lord Will Provide.' 'It may not be my way; it may not be thy way, but yet in His own way the Lord will provide.'"

Last year, after she had returned from a very delightful visit with us, she was not home a week before she sent a message of good cheer. It was truly a note of comfort that came from a loving heart.

Beloved friends in Hackettstown,
I greet you, one and all.
The kindness you have shown to me
My grateful thoughts recall;
The flowers that on my birthday came
I never will forget;
Within the garden of my heart
Those flowers are blooming yet.

Beloved pastor, called of God,
On Zion's walls to stand
And wield the mighty sword of truth
At His supreme command,—
I see you toiling at your post,
I hear your voice again,
I catch its well-remembered tones,
And, were I strong as then,
I'd speed away in joyful haste,
On airy pinions bright,
Where youthful lips will join to sing
My humble songs to-night.

And though I may not go to them,
I'll listen while they sing;
And as their music floats along
I'll hear its echoes ring;
And looking up in trusting faith,
Be this my glad refrain:
Our God be with you, precious ones,
Until we meet again.

And now she has passed on to the Land of Pure Delight of which she sang so beautifully and so often. Yet she is not dead. Her memory lingers in the hearts of those who knew and loved her and on whom the rays of her sunshine fell; while amid that larger circle, the wide world over, who knew Fanny Crosby only through her ministry of song, her name and her influence are among those things which men and women of this and succeeding generations will not willingly let die.

II

Childhood

Jesus dear, I come to Thee,
  Thou hast said I may;
Tell me what my life should be,
  Take my sins away;
Jesus dear, I learn of Thee
  In Thy Word divine;
Every promise there I see,
  May I call it mine.

Jesus dear, I long for Thee,
  Long Thy peace to know;
Grant those purer joys to me
  Earth can ne'er bestow;
Jesus dear, I cling to Thee.
  When my heart is sad
Thou wilt kindly speak to me,
  Thou wilt made me glad.

Jesus dear, I trust in Thee,
  Trust Thy tender love;
There's a happy home for me
  With Thy saints above;
Jesus, I would come to Thee,
  Thou hast said I may;
Tell me what my life should be,
  Take my sins away.

II

CHILDHOOD

"Hers was the line of noble souls and pure,
Of patient doers well, dear friends of God,
Who faithful e'en through suffering could endure,
Walking the way the saints and martyrs trod."

IT was in the year 1895 that Aunt Fanny Crosby first came to our home. Thus began a friendship that was to so bind its golden cords of love around our lives as to enable us to feel them drawing us to the best and highest things, even though she has herself entered the realms of the blest.

After ten years' acquaintance, I felt free to talk with Aunt Fanny, who was looked for at our home just as we look for spring and fall. In the glow of the evening we sat together in the month of

May. It was a charming sunset, and I endeavoured to describe it to her. She clapped her hands and cried, "Glorious, glorious."

"Aunt Fanny," I said, "I have read much about your life right from my childhood days, and since, as you say, you expect to live to be one hundred and three I want you to give me, from your own heart, the story of your life. Each time you visit us we will take some particular phase."

The birch was burning brightly in the open fireplace as we sat together that evening, and as I drew my chair towards hers she dropped her knitting in her lap and said, "You dear soul, I have been thinking of what you asked me at sundown, and I shall be as happy as a lark to tell you anything that would be of vital interest to other lives to help them along the rugged path. Mine has been an experience that has ripened into a faith as strong as the hills. It has given me a hope that admits me into the room called Beautiful. It has arrayed my pathway with the jewels of love so that in my old age I love everybody.

"Now, to begin. I was born on the twenty-fourth day of March in the year of our Lord 1820 in Southeast, Putnam County, New York. The cottage in which I was born was only one story high. My mother was a brave, industrious woman of the New England type that helped to lay the foundation of this Republic. My father's name was John Crosby. I have no recollection of him, for he died before I was twelve months old, but we traced the Crosbys back to 1635, when they lived beyond the Charles River, and were among the founders of Harvard College. So you see I belong to a granite stock. Our family, too, was noted for its longevity. My mother lived to be ninety-one, my great-grandmother reached the age of one hundred and three, and I would like to go a little beyond that.

"When about six weeks old I was taken sick and my eyes grew very weak and those who had charge of me poulticed my eyes. Their lack of knowledge and skill destroyed my sight forever. As I grew older they told me I should never see the faces of my friends, the flowers of the field, the blue of the skies, or the golden beauty of the stars.

"When my dear mother knew that I was to be shut out from all the beauties of the natural world she told me, in my girlhood, that two of the world's greatest poets were blind, and that sometimes Providence deprived persons of some physical faculty in order that the spiritual insight might more fully awake. I remember well the day she read to me, with deep expression, Milton's sonnet on his blindness:

" 'When I consider how my light is spent
Ere half my days, in this dark world and wide;
And that one talent which is death to hide,
Lodged with me useless, though my soul more bent
To serve therewith my Maker, and present
My true account, lest He turning chide;
Doth God exact day labour, light denied,
I fondly ask? But patience, to prevent
That murmur, soon replies, God doth not need
Either man's work or his own gifts; who best
Bear His mild yoke, they serve Him best; His state
Is kingly; thousands at His bidding speed
And post o'er land and ocean without rest;
They also serve who only stand and wait.'

"Soon I learned what other children possessed, but I made up my mind to store away a little jewel in my heart, which I called Content. This has been the comfort of my whole life. When I was eight years of age I wrote:

O what a happy soul am I!
Although I cannot see,
I am resolved that in this world
Contented I will be.

How many blessings I enjoy,
That other people don't.
To weep and sigh because I'm blind,
I cannot, and I won't.

"I was a child of deep affection and a great lover of pets. One evening my mother brought home a motherless lamb and I said, 'Mother, I'll be a little mother to that little creature. I'll call it Fanny's little lamb.' Right there mother sat down and told me, for the first time, the story of *Mary's Little Lamb*. I shall never forget it. I could see in my mind's eye Mary going to school with her pet lamb; so I made up my mind that I would love *my* lamb. I played with it and took it with me wherever I went. We grew up together, the lamb and I. We roamed the fields, we went over the hills, we ram-

Where Fanny Crosby was born

bled down by the brook, and often fell asleep together under an old oak tree. One day my heart was broken. Mother sold my pet to a butcher, and I wept bitter tears. They never told me what they did with my friend and companion, but at nights before I went to bed I would kneel down and cry and ask God to bless Fanny's lamb.

"My grandmother was to me more than I can ever express by word or pen. When she knew that her little granddaughter was to be sightless for life, she sought to make up for the loss of my eyes by coming to our home, taking me on her knee and rocking me while she told me of the beautiful sun, with its sunrise and its sunset. And she never overlooked its noonday splendour. Of the shining moon she gave me such descriptions as I never forgot. The golden stars were so described by her as to give me a love for astronomy that continues to the present hour. The clouds with their shapes and colours were made real to me by her. One afternoon after a thunder-storm Grandma caught me in her arms and took me to the brow of a hill and described a beautiful rainbow overarching the Croton River. I remember her saying, 'O Fanny, there is such a beautiful bow in the heavens. It has seven colours; I wish you could see it; it is a sign of God's covenant of mercy to this world.' She described the colours in such vivid language that they were all real to me.

"She also told me the story of the birds. I knew the red-headed woodpecker, the red-winged blackbird, the mocking-bird with its white chin, and the bird with its garment of blue. One day I heard a strange sound coming from the meadow saying, 'Whippoorwill.' Grandma told me about the bird which gave out that curious note and described its mottled wings and reddish brown breast and its bristled mouth, with its white bristled tail. So, afterwards, whenever I heard the sound of the whippoorwill I knew its colour and its shape. From Grandmother I also learned something of the meadow-lark, the cuckoo, the song-sparrow, the goldfinch, the yellow warbler, the wren, and the robin. I grew to know the birds by their songs. One day I wrote of the bird:

Ah, now thou art happy again, my bird,
And thy voice rings out so clear,
That the robin, the wren, and the bluebird, too,
Are coming its trill to hear.

"Grandma was also my teacher in flowers. Flowers always had a charm for me. I loved to handle them, and I revelled in their fragrance. She told me of the apple, cherry and peach blossoms. She described the pansy, the peony, the sweet pea, the scarlet poppy, the primrose, and roses, pink, red, white, and yellow. Often we went down to the brook together to gather violets. The violet with its fragrance and its modesty is my favourite flower. I once wrote a poem on seeking violets. Here is part of it:

> Roaming all day in the meadow so green,
> Seeking for violets, thou art, my queen,
> Where have you hid them? Down deep in your heart?
> Why are you blushing? And why do you start?
> Seeking for violets? When do they grow?
> Think you to find them in summer? No, no;
> Not such a thought ever entered your head,
> Nor is there truth in a word you have said.

"Often in the fall season Grandma took me for walks over the hills and through the lanes, telling me the story of the trees and their leaves. I knew the trees by the sense of touch and by their fragrance, and the leaves by handling and remembering. I often gathered the autumn leaves and played with them. In after years I wrote some verses entitled, 'Only a Leaf.'

'Tis only a leaf, a withered leaf,
But its story is fraught with pain;
'Twas the gift of one who is far away,
And will never come back again.

"It was Grandma who brought the Bible to me, and me to the Bible. The stories of the Holy Book came from her lips and entered my heart and took deep root there. When the evening shadows fell, Grandma would take me alone, and rocking me in her old chair, tell me of a kind heavenly Father, who sent His only son Jesus Christ down into this world to be a Saviour and a Friend to all mankind. Then she taught me to kneel in prayer and often I bowed my weary little head and sightless eyes in Grandma's lap, and fell asleep.

"Years ago I dedicated a few verses to the memory of Grandma's rocking-chair and I often repeat them wherever I have an opportunity to speak in public:

> I am thinking of a cottage,
> On a quiet rural dell,
> And a brook that ran beside it,
> That I used to love so well.
> I have sat for hours and listened,
> While it rippled at my feet,
> And I thought no other music
> In the world was half so sweet."

Here Aunt Fanny said, "I wish you would bring me the Bible. I want you to read the thirty-second and thirty-third chapters of the book of Deuteronomy." I read them to her as her face gleamed with the very sunshine of God. Clapping her hands together she said, "I look upon these as my favourite chapters in the Old Testament. Where in all literature can we find such expressions of beauty and vitality? This Holy Book nurtured my early life. When a girl I could repeat from memory the five books of Moses, most of the New Testament, many of the Psalms, the Proverbs of Solomon, the Book of Ruth, and that greatest of all prose poems, the Songs of Solomon. Most of my early poetry was built up on subjects taken from the Bible, such as: 'The Trial of Abraham's Faith,' 'The Meeting of Jacob and Joseph,' 'Samson and the Philistines.' The New Testament gave me many subjects of great value for poems. To-day I love the dear Old Book, that I have tested and tried, more than ever. 'The statutes of the Lord are right.' I have proved them. Through all my years they have always been 'Yea,' and 'Amen.' You know that to one like myself shut in from much that those blessed with the sense of seeing enjoy, God's Holy Word has been, and is, doubly precious. On it I have rested right through the years. On it I rest now; and whether my years on earth be few or many, I shall rest on it to the end.

I wrote a little poem for Mr. I. Allan Sankey not so long since, which relates my love for the Bible:

> O Book, that with rev'rence I honour,
>   What joy in thy pages I see!
> O Book of my childhood devotion,
>   More precious than rubies to me."

The birch logs in the open fireplace had by this time burned to ashes, and little shimmering mounds lit up with fire opals were flinging their glow over their beds of silver, as Aunt Fanny and I parted for the night.

III

Growing Into Womanhood

Hold Thou my hand; so weak am I, and helpless,
  I dare not take one step without Thy aid;
Hold Thou my hand; for then, O loving Saviour,
  No dread of ill shall make my soul afraid.

Hold Thou my hand, and closer, closer, draw me
  To Thy dear self—my hope, my joy, my all;
Hold Thou my hand, lest haply I should wander,
  And missing Thee, my trembling feet should fall.

Hold Thou my hand; the way is dark before me
  Without the sunlight of Thy face divine;
But when by faith I catch its radiant glory,
  What heights of joy, what rapturous songs, are mine.

Hold Thou my hand, that, when I reach the margin
  Of that lone river Thou didst cross for me,
A heavenly light may flash along its waters,
  And every wave like crystal bright shall be.

[*1874*]

III

GROWING INTO WOMANHOOD

"Friendship, peculiar boon of heaven,
The noble mind's delight and pride,
To men and angels only given,
To all the lower world denied."

"AUNT FANNY," I said, "I want you to take up the thread of your life-story just where you left it last spring."

"Well," she replied, "I am ready."

It was the fall of the year and Aunt Fanny was again at our fireside. On the Sabbath she had thrilled the hearts of hundreds of people with her message. On Monday afternoon I took her for a long auto ride in the country, with the understanding that we were to spend the evening together in the study. I took the little rocking-chair, which we always kept for her, to the study and as she entered I described to her the pictures that hung on the walls. They were of Tennyson, of Browning, and Carlyle, of Newman, Ruskin, Lincoln. As she sat down I told her that just over her head was Hoffman's picture of Christ, and in front of her the faces of Florence Nightingale, Harriet Beecher Stowe, Julia Ward Howe, and Jenny Lind. "Have you Jenny Lind's picture?" she said. "I heard her sing; I will tell you about her later."

Aunt Fanny seemed to be as one inspired when she realized that she was surrounded by so many faces of those whose lives and works she knew so well.

After a little while she said: "Now, we will go on with my story. When I was about nine years of age we went to live at Ridgefield, Connecticut. Here we spent six most beautiful and beneficial years. It was here that I first met Sylvester Main, father of Hubert P. Main, who in after life became one of my most precious friends. At the age of fifteen I entered the Institution for the Blind in New York City, where I remained as a pupil for twelve years, improving my opportunities and stocking my mind with useful knowledge. At the Institution I made a careful study of the poetry of Thomas Moore, Horatius Bonar, James Montgomery, Longfellow, Tennyson, Bryant, Whittier, Willis, Wesley, Morris and many others. Here also I wrote many poems, unknown to my teachers. One long poem on the poets, however, was praised by my friends. It concludes,

> You from whose garners I have gleaned
> Such precious fruit, the task has seemed
> So pleasant that my humble pen
> Would fain resume its work again;
> In your bright realms 'twere bliss to stay;
> But time forbids, and I obey.

"While in this Institution I was often taken to churches and schools to show what the blind were capable of doing.

Well do I remember our visiting Congress in the autumn of 1843 when I recited a number of my poems, which were well received. They told me that stalwart men were moved to tears when in one of my poems I reached the words:

> O ye who here from every state convene,
> Illustrious band, may we not hope the scene
> That you behold will prove to every mind
> Instruction hath a ray to cheer the blind.

"On returning from such visits a deeper inner longing awoke within my breast for the crystal streams of literature and the friendship of faithful souls. I wanted to go with the gallant, to sit with the sincere, to associate with those who, like myself, were winning their way, in the face of the fiercest foes, seeking a truer meaning to life. A great life was a wonderful inspiration to me. Whenever an opportunity came to meet noted statesmen, masterful musicians, literary leaders and artistic mortals, I always availed myself of it. I craved for them as the heart panteth for the water-brooks.

"To know and make friends with the builders of this nation was a desire of my growing womanhood. Just think, I have lived during the lifetime of all the Presidents of the United States, Washington excepted. Ex-President John Adams was called to rest in the year 1826. I was then just six years old.

"When in Washington I listened with untold pleasure to John Quincy Adams, the sixth President of the Republic. I admired his firmness, intelligence and integrity. He had a warm corner in my heart. I was also a true lover and supporter of Andrew Jackson. He was a man of principle and fought for his nation and not his position. He was a big man, and I honoured him and used all the influence I possessed in his favour. Though we never met face to face, he knew my strong feelings towards him.

President VanBuren I met, talked with, supped with and hailed as the 'Little Magician.' Down to his dying day he was one of my closest friends. President William Henry Harrison, who remained in office only one month, I revered. I was glad to sing his deeds and herald his virtues in song:

> The forest with his praises rung,
> His fame was echoed far and wide,
> With loud hurrah his name was sung,
> Columbia's hero and her pride.
> The tuneful harp is now unstrung,
> And on the drooping willow hung.

"When President John Tyler visited the Institution for the Blind in New York City, I was asked to write a poem of welcome and recite it for him. I did my very best and when I concluded with the words

> And the glad song of our nation shall be,
> Hurrah for John Tyler and liberty tree,

the people clapped their hands and gave

me such an ovation that I shall never forget his visit. President James Knox Polk was my intimate personal friend. I recited for him at the White House, and he became unusually interested in me. In the year 1848 President Polk visited the Institution for the Blind and I had the honour of dining with him. Then he took my arm, and we went out under the lofty trees and through the grounds where we conversed together and listened to the bluebirds and robins. For a simple kindness which I showed to a domestic the President said, 'You have done well; I commend you for it. Kindness to those in the humblest capacity of life should be our rule of conduct. By this act you have won, not only my respect, but my esteem.' On leaving him I went to my room feeling as happy as a bird in spring time that I had communed with a great scholar and statesman. That night, ere sleep closed my eyelids, I breathed a petition to our merciful Father to cause His face to shine upon my friend President Polk.

"One of the most sympathetic and dramatic scenes through which I passed during my stay at the Institution, was when Henry Clay came to visit us. I knew the struggle of his early boyhood, and the story of his conquest over difficulties was an inspiration to my life. I was chosen to recite a poem of welcome in his honour. After I had rendered it, he came and took me by the hand and said to the audience, 'This is not the only poem for which I am indebted to this lady. Six months ago she sent me some lines on the death of my dear son.' Here both Henry Clay and myself broke down and wept.

"I have been greatly interested in all our Presidents, but, to me, Lincoln towers above the rest like a lofty cedar, and his name will never be effaced from the annals of the world's history. In reading carefully the history of great men, Abraham Lincoln is my captain and leader. Grant, Hayes, and Garfield have a secure place in my memory and a warm spot in my heart, but it was with Grover Cleveland that I was brought into closer touch than with any other of the Presidents. He was secretary to the Institution for the Blind and I often went to him with my heartaches, and he always proved a sympathetic friend. He copied for me very many of my poems. Through all the years he knew me he took an interest in my life and work. I have visited him at his home in Lakewood and at Princeton. A few years ago he wrote me a letter of which I will send you a copy."

[This is the letter :]

"*My Dear Friend :*

"It is more than fifty years ago that our acquaintance and friendship began ; and ever since that time I have watched your continuous and disinterested labour in uplifting humanity, and pointing out the way to an appreciation of God's goodness and mercy.

"Though those labours have, I know, brought you abundant rewards in your consciousness of good accomplished, those who have known of your works and sympathized with your noble purposes owe it to themselves that you are apprized of their remembrance of these things. I am, therefore, exceedingly gratified to learn that your eighty-fifth birthday is to be celebrated with demonstration of this remembrance. As one proud to call you an old friend, I desire to be early in congratulating you on your long life of usefulness, and wishing you in the years yet to be added to you the peace and comfort born of the love of God.

"Yours very sincerely,
"GROVER CLEVELAND."

The clock in the church tower was striking eleven as my wife brought in a cup of tea for Aunt Fanny. She drank it and added as she wished me good-night, "To-morrow I will tell you a little love story."

IV

A Little Love Story

'Tis only a leaf, a withered leaf,
  But its story is fraught with pain;
'Twas the gift of one who is far away
  And will never return again;
'Tis only a leaf, a withered leaf
  And yet I prize it so,
For it brings to my mem'ry the brightest hour
  I ever on earth shall know.

'Tis only a leaf, a withered leaf,
  But its story is fraught with pain;
'Twas the gift of one who is far away
  And will never return again;
He will never return; but I feel ere long
  My spirit with his will be,
And the old-time love shall be sweeter there
  Where I know that he waits for me.

IV

A LITTLE LOVE STORY

"Music, religious heat inspires,
It wakes the soul and lifts it high,
And wings it with sublime desires,
And fits it to bespeak the Deity."

"AUNT FANNY, I hope you are not too tired after so long a ride to tell me the story you promised last night?"

It had been a charming Indian summer day, and Aunt Fanny had been taken for an auto ride through New Brunswick and Princeton. When told in the morning of the proposed trip she jumped up and danced around the room in rare delight. She truly loved an auto ride at any time, but what filled her heart with special glee was the fact that she was to visit two college towns where she had so many faithful friends.

We had spent a glorious day, and were back at the manse. Aunt Fanny sat rocking in her little armchair, her knitting needle and cotton in her lap ready to begin a wash-rag for the lady of the house.

She plied her needles for a little while after I put my question and then with a smile began:

"When they told me at the Institution for the Blind that William Cullen Bryant was coming to address the students and teachers, sweet music filled my soul; for I had read most of his poems and knew many of them by heart. He had been kind enough to read several of my poems and had written me encouraging me to continue writing verse. I cannot tell you how much Bryant's words helped me when I felt disheartened or discouraged. He knew the secret of the art of a kind word. I too have made it a point in my life to help as far as it lay in my power those who were struggling to reach the summit.

"Right from the time when I first heard of P. T. Barnum I was very much interested in the man, and when I read that he was to bring Jenny Lind, the Swedish nightingale, to this country I became feverish to hear her. Words cannot express my feelings when the superintendent announced that Jenny Lind was to sing before the students and faculty of the Institution for the Blind. My heart was like an overflowing cup, my joy a living fountain, my body light as a feather. That morning I was unable to eat any breakfast. Jenny Lind was to sing, and I to recite my poem, 'The Swedish Nightingale.' I felt her presence as she came on the platform and as I rose to speak I felt her influence all about me. I concluded my poem with

> Yet, Sweden's daughter, thou shalt live
> In every grateful heart;
> And may the choicest gifts of heaven
> Be thine, where'er thou art.

"I have heard many of the world's greatest singers but no other has made such a lasting impression upon my mind as Jenny Lind singing, 'Home, Home, Sweet, Sweet Home.'

"In this connection I must tell you of my visit to, and friendship with, Ole Bull. He was ten years my senior, and born in Bergen, Norway. Having heard a great deal about his wonderful playing on the violin, I, like other girls, was wild to hear him play. When it was announced that Ole Bull was to pay us a visit, you can just imagine how I felt. I can weep over it even now. It seemed as though I literally *saw* him, as he drew his bow over the strings of his violin. The birds sang, the brooks rippled, the rain fell, the thunder roared, the sunbeams danced, the bells pealed, the angels sang. We were all enchanted. Burning tears of joy coursed down my cheeks and a light celestial threw its halo over my brow. When I grasped the hand of Ole Bull I felt as if I were touching one from another world. We sat down together. He talked with me and his words charmed and cheered me. He gave me a clearer vision of life and love than I had ever conceived, and his music has made my own songs more sweet, more divine.

"Now for my little love story. Some people seem to forget that blind girls have just as great a faculty for loving and *do* love just as much and just as truly as those who have their sight. I had a heart that was hungry for love. When I was about twenty a gifted young man by the name of Alexander Van Alstyne came to our Institution. He also was blind, and a most talented student. He was fond of classic literature and theological lore, but made music a specialty. After hearing several of my poems he became deeply interested in my work; and I after listening to his sweet strains of music became interested in him. Thus we soon grew to be very much concerned for each other. One day in June he went out under the elm trees to listen to the birds sing, and the winds play their love-song among the leaves. It was here the voice of love spoke within his breast. Listening, he heard its voice of music trilling its notes to his heart. Just then another to whom the voice was calling came towards the spot where he was musing. I placed my right hand on his left and called him 'Van.' Then it was that two happy lovers sat in silence while the sunbeams danced around their heads, and the golden curtains of day drew in their light. 'Van' took up the harp of love, and drawing his fingers over the golden chords, sang to me the song of a true lover's heart. From that hour two lives looked on a new universe, for love met love, and all the world was changed. We were no longer blind, for the light of love showed us where the lilies bloomed, and where the crystal waters find the moss-mantled spring.

"On March the fifth in the year 1858 we were united in marriage. Now I am going to tell you of something that only my closest friends know. I became a mother and knew a mother's love. God gave us a tender babe but the angels came down and took our infant up to God and to His throne.

"Van went home to his Father's house in the year 1902. During my stay as a teacher in the Institution for the Blind I touched the poetic garment of Mrs. Sigourney, sat long at the feet of Bayard Taylor, slaked my thirsty soul at the living streams of Frances Ridley Havergal, and drank deeply from the chalices of Longfellow, Whittier, Holmes, and Lowell. During these years I heard the best in music and read the purest in poetry and prose. This has of course helped me in my own work. From the master singers of my own country I have gathered inspiration for my own writing, and whatever my hymns have helped to do in the world has been much stimulated by my having sat at the feet of the great ones in the temple of song."

The hour had now grown late and I saw that Aunt Fanny had grown tired, and that the hour for retirement was near. With her usual cup of tea she went to her room, promising on the morrow to relate the story of how she became a writer of sacred songs.

V

How I Became a Hymn-Writer

We are going, we are going
  To a home beyond the skies,
Where the fields are robed in beauty
  And the sunlight never dies;
Where the fount of life is flowing
  In the valley green and fair,
We shall dwell in love together;
  There will be no parting there.

We are going, we are going,
  And the music we have heard
Like the echo of the woodland,
  Or the carol of a bird;
With the rosy light of morning,
  On the calm and fragrant air,
Still it murmurs, softly murmurs,
  There will be no parting there.

We are going, we are going,
  When the day of life is o'er,
To the pure and happy region
  Where our friends have gone before
They are singing with the angels
  In that land so bright and fair;
We shall dwell with them forever;
  There will be no parting there.

[*1864—Fanny Crosby's first hymn.*]

V

HOW I BECAME A HYMN-WRITER

" Such songs have power to quiet
The restless pulse of care,
And come like the benediction
That follows after prayer."

"VERY early in life I began to write bits of verse," said Aunt Fanny. We sat together, the blind singer and I, just as the evening bells were calling to worship, she relating the story of how she became a hymn-writer. "From my eighth year I can remember little poetic pictures forming themselves in my mind. When I gathered flowers and caught their fragrance I wanted to say something poetic about them. When I heard the birds sing, I was anxious to understand their notes.

As I wandered down by the brook with my grandmother, listening to the rippling of the waters, I felt something in my soul that I wanted to say about the rivulet and the river.

"On entering the Institution for the Blind I knew many poems by heart and had already cultivated a strong love for the poetic art. My teachers did not encourage me to write poetry; often they would take from me my poetic works. This grieved my heart. One day Dr. Combe of Boston came to examine our *craniums*. As he touched my head, and looked into my face he remarked, 'And here is a poetess; give her every possible encouragement. Read the best books to her, and teach her to appreciate the finest there is in poetry. You will hear from this young lady some day.'

"This was as music to my soul. I had waited long for some one to encourage me to adhere to what I already felt was to be my life-work—hymn-writing. I had written a large number of secular and religious poems, a few cantatas and many songs, but my real writing of Christian hymns began on my leaving the Institute, and becoming associated with some notable religious characters. They have been everything to me. Many of them have reached the Golden Strand, and I am sure of meeting and knowing them there.

"Mr. W. B. Bradbury I first met at 425 Broome Street, New York City. He asked me if I would write a hymn for him. I was delighted. I was hungry for some one to ask me that question. In three days I returned with some verses which he set to music and published. This was my first hymn:

> We are going, we are going,
> To a home beyond the skies,
> Where the fields are robed in beauty,
> And the sunlight never dies.

We are going, we are going,
And the music we have heard,
Like the echo of the woodland,
Or the carol of the bird.

"My real work as a hymn-writer began from that hour. I had found my mission, and was the happiest creature in all the land. Mr. Bradbury lightened many of my darkest days and scattered sunshine over my hours of care.

"My hymn which first won world-wide attention was, 'Pass Me Not, O Gentle Saviour.' Mr. W. H. Doane, who became a very dear friend of mine, suggested the subject to me. It was written in the year 1868. Dear Mr. Sankey said, 'No hymn in our collection was more popular than this one at the meetings in London in 1874. It was sung at almost every service, in Her Majesty's Theatre, Pall Mall.' This hymn has been translated into many foreign languages, and remains a favourite wherever the English tongue

Fanny Crosby as she was in 1872

is spoken. Mr. Doane did very much to bring my songs to the front. One day he came to me and said, 'Fanny, I have a tune I would like to have you write words for.' He played it over and I exclaimed, 'That says, Safe in the Arms of Jesus.' I went to my room, and in about thirty minutes I returned with the hymn that has since been a comfort and a solace to many heavy, sorrowing hearts.

> Safe in the arms of Jesus,
> Safe on His gentle breast,
> There by His love o'ershaded,
> Sweetly my soul shall rest.
> Hark, 'tis the voice of angels,
> Borne in a song to me,
> Over the fields of glory,
> Over the jasper sea.

"Dr. John Hall, in his day the famous pastor of Fifth Avenue Presbyterian Church, New York, once told me that 'Safe in the Arms of Jesus' gave more peace and satisfaction to mothers, who had lost their children, than any other hymn he had ever known. It has become famous throughout the world and was one of the first of American hymns to be translated into foreign languages.

"Among my first and foremost friends, —one whose memory to me is as ointnent poured forth—was Sylvester Main, of the firm of Biglow and Main. He became interested in me when a girl in Ridgefield, Connecticut. He was my faithful counsellor and guide. His son, Hubert P. Main, has always been as a brother to me, and I have known him for a half-century. He wrote the music for my words:

> On the banks beyond the river
> We shall meet no more to sever;
> In the bright, the bright forever,
> In the summer-land of song.

"Theodore E. Perkins, Philip Phillips, Dr. Robert Lowry, Dr. Van Meter, P. P.

Bliss, James M. McGranahan, Mrs. Joseph F. Knapp—all these I knew. But no names are so sacred to me as those of Dwight L. Moody, Ira D. Sankey, George C. Stebbins, and William H. Doane. This nation has not produced a company of stronger men, nor any who have worked harder for the betterment of mankind. I must say a few words about dear Mr. Moody, for he meant so much to me. I never knew or found a kinder, bigger-hearted man. I look upon his life as simply wonderful. He was the biggest piece of humanity this nation has yet produced.

"Then there was my never-failing friend, Ira D. Sankey. I could give you a whole bookful about him. I was with him so much. He put new life into many of my songs. I revere his memory. The last time I visited him in his home in Brooklyn we went over together the manifold mercies of our God. It was really pathetic to know that that stalwart man was lying on his bed—sightless. We wept and sang and prayed together. He never expected to cross over the river before Aunt Fanny, so on one occasion he wrote me a beautiful letter saying: 'I wish that when you get to heaven (as you may before I shall) that you will watch for me at the pearly gate at the eastern side of the city; and when I get there I'll take you by the hand and lead you along the golden street, up to the throne of God, and there we'll stand before the Lamb, and say to Him: "And now we see Thee face to face, saved by Thy matchless, boundless grace, and we are satisfied."'

"One of my most devoted and precious friends is George C. Stebbins. He gave wings to my poem 'Saved by Grace.' If ever there was a man of high honour and culture of character, it is Mr. Stebbins. He has filled up every nook of my life with his goodness. I was seventy-one years of age when I wrote 'Saved by Grace.' I sent it to The Biglow & Main Co. They paid me for it, and placed it in their safe with hundreds of other hymns. Three years after I was visiting Mr. Sankey at East Northfield, Mass., while attending the summer conferences. One evening Mr. Sankey asked me to give a short address. I tried to excuse myself, as I did not feel prepared to speak before so many notables. Mr. Sankey, however, would not take 'no' for an answer. So I did as he requested, and there must have been a Providence in it after all, for I closed my remarks with the words of my hymn:

> Some day the silver cord will break,
>   And I no more as now shall sing;
> But, O, the joy when I shall wake
>   Within the palace of the King!

"When I had finished Mr. Sankey

turned to me and said, 'Fanny, where did you get that beautiful hymn?' 'Why, you ought to know,' I replied; 'I sold that song to you three years ago, and have waited all this time for an opportunity to recite it.' Mr. Sankey lost no time in obtaining a copy of the song and requested Mr. Stebbins to set it to music, which he did, with the result that 'Saved by Grace' has become one of my most popular and useful hymns.

"Mr. Sankey's son, Ira Allan Sankey, now president of The Biglow & Main Co., has taken his sainted father's place, and has written some very impressive music for some of my songs. I was at a certain church a little while ago, and heard the soloist sing 'Grandma's Rocking Chair,' set to music by I. Allan Sankey, and I really thought the son had surpassed the father in sweetness of tone and harmony of expression. On the same evening the congregation sang my hymn, 'Never Give Up' (music by the same composer), and I was delighted with the work of the son of the man who made 'The Ninety and Nine' famous. To this day I can hear the strains as the people sang my words that night:

Never be sad or desponding
 If thou hast faith to believe;
Grace, for the duties before thee,
 Ask of thy God and receive.

Never give up, never give up,
Never give up to thy sorrows,
 Jesus will bid them depart.
Trust in the Lord, trust in the Lord,
Sing when your trials are greatest,
 Trust in the Lord and take heart.

"There is a great and wonderful truth embodied in these words. The whole victory of life is in them—'Trust in the Lord and take heart.' That means the exercise of courage, the consciousness of being linked to One mightier than our-selves, and it helps one to keep smiling, to keep sunshiny, and to have, not only a song on the lip, but one in the heart."

VI

My Living Hymns

Rescue the Perishing

Rescue the perishing,
Care for the dying,
Snatch them in pity from sin and the grave;
Weep o'er the erring one,
Lift up the fallen,
Tell them of Jesus, the mighty to save.

Rescue the perishing,
Care for the dying:
Jesus is merciful,
Jesus will save.

Though they are slighting Him,
Still He is waiting,
Waiting the penitent child to receive:
Plead with them earnestly,
Plead with them gently:
He will forgive if they only believe.

Down in the human heart,
Crushed by the tempter,
Feelings lie buried that grace can restore:
Touched by a loving heart,
Wakened by kindness,
Chords that were broken will vibrate once more.

Rescue the perishing;
Duty demands it:
Strength for thy labour the Lord will provide:
Back to the narrow way
Patiently win them:
Tell the poor wanderer a Saviour has died.

[*1869*]

VI

MY LIVING HYMNS

> "Such songs have power to quiet
> The restless pulse of care,
> And come like the benediction
> That follows after prayer."

"AUNT FANNY," I said, "I wish you would tell me the story of the five hymns by which you are most widely known."

"Bless your dear soul," she replied in her usual ready way, "I shall be delighted to do so."

The immediate cause of my asking for an account of how her greatest successes came to be written was my receiving a new hymnal which contained the names of fifty-three women authors, with eighty-three hymns to their credit. Frances Ridley Havergal had written eight songs for the book, Charlotte Elliott, six, Fanny Crosby, five. Three of the writers were born the same year as herself,—Anna L. Waring, who wrote "In Heavenly Love Abiding," Anna D. Warner, known by "One More Day's Work for Jesus," and Alice Cary. Of the rest she at least knew the names, and in most cases something more. We talked of many of these authors and then I put my question.

"The first I must tell you of is 'Rescue the Perishing.' It was written in the year 1869, when I was forty-nine years old. It has been placed among the 'One Hundred Hymns You Ought to Know.' Many of my hymns were written after experiences in New York mission work. This one was thus written. I was addressing a large company of working men one hot summer evening, when the thought kept forcing itself on my mind that some mother's boy must be rescued that night or not at all. So I made a pressing plea that if there were a boy present who had wandered from his mother's home and teaching, he would come to me at the close of the service. A young man of eighteen came forward and said, 'Did you mean me? I promised my mother to meet her in heaven, but as I am now living that will be impossible.' We prayed for him and he finally arose with a new light in his eyes and exclaimed in triumph: 'Now I can meet my mother in heaven, for I have found God.'

"A few days before Mr. Doane had sent me the subject, 'Rescue the Perishing,' and while I sat there that evening, the line came to me, 'Rescue the Perishing, care for the dying.' I could think of nothing else that night. When I arrived home I went to work on the hymn at once, and before I retired it was ready for the melody. The next day my song was written out and forwarded to Mr. Doane, who wrote the beautiful and touching music as it now stands to my hymn.

> Rescue the perishing,
> Care for the dying,
> Snatch them in pity from sin and the grave;
> Weep o'er the erring one,
> Lift up the fallen,
> Tell them of Jesus the mighty to save.

"In the year 1873 I wrote 'Blessed Assurance.' My friend Mrs. Joseph F. Knapp composed a melody and played it over to me two or three times on the piano. She then asked what it said. I replied:

> Blessed assurance, Jesus is mine!
> O what a foretaste of glory divine!
> Heir of salvation, purchase of God,
> Born of His spirit, washed in His blood.

"Mr. Sankey in his 'Story of the Gospel Hymns' says, 'One of the most popular and useful of the Gospel Hymns is

"Blessed Assurance." It was sung by a large delegation of Christian Endeavourers on the train going to Minneapolis some years ago, and made a lasting impression upon many of the passengers. The people of Minneapolis, too, were greatly delighted with the Christian Endeavourers as they sang this song on the way to Convention Hall.'

"Towards the close of a day in the year 1874 I was sitting in my room thinking of the nearness of God through Christ as the constant companion of my pilgrim journey, when my heart burst out with the words:

> Thou, my everlasting portion,
> More than friend or life to Thee;
> All along my pilgrim journey,
> Saviour, let me walk with Thee.

"Mr. Doane sent me the subject and the tune of 'Saviour, More Than Life to Me' or 'Every Day and Hour,' requesting me to write a hymn on that theme. This I did in the year 1874. This hymn has given me great comfort and joy in my saddest moments. I know that God has blessed this hymn to tens of thousands of souls. Whenever I hear it sung it strengthens my faith, fires my hope and feeds my love.

> Saviour, more than life to me,
> I am clinging, clinging close to Thee;
> Let Thy precious blood applied
> Keep me ever near Thy side.
>
> Every day, every hour,
> Let me feel Thy cleansing power;
> May Thy tender love to me
> Bind me closer, closer, Lord to Thee.

"I do not want you to think," continued Aunt Fanny, "that while I love my own songs and want them to be useful that I disregard the hymns of the great writers of the Church. Many of them are engraven on my memory. I would go short of a meal any time to hear the lines of Charles Wesley, or Cowper, Watts, Montgomery, Bonar, Keble, Newton, Toplady, Heber, and Faber. This last author has written my favourite hymn :

> " 'Faith of our fathers living still
> In spite of dungeon, fire, and sword :
> O how our hearts beat high with joy
> Whene'er we hear that glorious word !
> Faith of our fathers ! holy faith !
> We will be true to thee till death !'

"There is a great hymn written by a minister in Scotland," added Fanny, "whose name is George Matheson. He has written many wonderful books ; but it is his verse that attracts me most. Some of his poems are really fine, while 'O Love That Wilt Not Let Me Go' is a really great hymn. After it was first read to me I was informed that its author was a blind man. I made up my mind to learn it by heart. It is truly a great hymn.

" 'O Love that wilt not let me go,
I rest my weary soul in thee;
I give thee back the life I owe,
That in thine ocean depths its flow
May richer, fuller be.

* * * *

" 'O Cross that liftest up my head,
I dare not ask to fly from thee;
I lay in dust life's glory dead,
And from the ground there blossoms red
Life that shall endless be.' "

Here the lunch bell rang and Aunt Fanny tripped down-stairs as nimbly as a girl in her teens blithely singing:

Saviour, more than life to me,
I am clinging, clinging close to Thee.

Up to the time when Aunt Fanny Crosby last visited my home, in her ninety-third year, she had written and had been paid for, by The Biglow & Main Co., five thousand nine hundred hymns. Mr. Hubert P. Main estimates that she has written for other publishers and friends two thousand seven hundred more, in ad-

Two Famous Hymn-Makers
Fanny Crosby and Ira D. Sankey

dition to secular poems. There is no doubt that altogether her hymns and poems total over eight thousand. While many of them may not be considered great, yet the majority have a mission of faith, of hope and love. In all probability not another person who ever lived has written so many sacred songs.

Their popularity has been unbounded. All over this broad land, as in countries across the seas, sweet-voiced singers have carried Fanny Crosby's gospel message in song. Moreover her lines have been sung by tens of thousands of believers never privileged to see in the flesh either the blind hymn-writer or the men who sang her verses all over two hemispheres. Some of these have gone, like Aunt Fanny, to sing a higher, nobler strain. Conspicuous among these stands the name of Ira D. Sankey. It is not easy, if indeed at all possible at this late date, to write anything fresh about the man whose name English-speaking people everywhere remember and revere. Under his singing of Fanny Crosby's hymns tens of thousands were brought to God. These hymns are sung to-day all over the wide world, and men and women catch anew their fervour and their power. Their message has gone forth in the earth, and from their proclamation has come help, solace and peace.

VII

Some Stories of My Songs

Pass me not, O gentle Saviour,
Hear my humble cry;
While on others Thou art smiling,
Do not pass me by.

Saviour, Saviour,
Hear my humble cry,
While on others Thou art calling,
Do not pass me by.

Let me at a throne of mercy
Find a sweet relief;
Kneeling there in deep contrition,
Help my unbelief.

Trusting only in Thy merit,
Would I seek Thy face;
Heal my wounded, broken spirit,
Save me by Thy grace.

Thou the Spring of all my comfort,
More than life to me,
Whom have I on earth beside Thee?
Whom in heaven but Thee?

[*1868*]

VII

SOME STORIES OF MY SONGS

"I think that life is not too long,
And therefore I determine
That many people read a song
Who will not read a sermon."

"DO you know that gentleman who has just left me?" asked Aunt Fanny.

"Slightly," I replied.

"Well, sit down," she continued; "there are fifteen minutes before the train leaves. I want to tell you what he has told me."

Some mutual friends had brought Aunt Fanny from Orange to Newark, and I was meeting her at the Pennsylvania Station. On my arrival I found her in conversation with a successful Christian business man of that city.

"'I am so pleased to see you,' this man said, 'for I have not met you since you were in England with Moody and Sankey.' He would hardly believe me when I told him I had never crossed the Atlantic. 'Well,' he insisted, 'if I didn't see you, I saw your spirit in your songs. In those days I was a young business man of good parents living in Leeds, Yorkshire. I took to drinking, and was going down fast, when I went to one of the Moody and Sankey Meetings and heard them sing, "Pass Me Not, O Gentle Saviour." I said in my heart, "I wish He would not pass *me* by." I went to the next night's meeting and the service began with the same hymn. I could resist no longer. There and then I fully surrendered my life to God. The next year I came to America, began business in this city, and have been successful. That is forty years ago. It is my custom to carry a copy of your hymn with me every day.' He bade me good-bye and before he went away placed this in my hand."

It was a bank note for twenty dollars.

On the train Fanny told me this story: "When in Orange I met a returned missionary who told me that many of my hymns were translated into the Chinese and Japanese languages, and that on one occasion, while he was visiting a missionary school in Korea, he met a little girl who was blind, whose name was Fanny. They called her 'Little Blind Fanny Crosby.' People often came a hundred and fifty miles to hear little blind Fanny sing,

> "Praise Him, praise Him, Jesus our Blessed
> Redeemer.
> Sing, O earth, His wonderful love proclaim.

"It was wonderful. He told me also that they knew 'Safe in the Arms of Jesus,' 'Blessed Assurance,' 'Rescue the Perishing' and 'Pass Me Not' in foreign-mission lands as well as in this country.

The last song that he heard in Korea was 'Saved by Grace,' sung by little blind Fanny."

In September, 1907, Aunt Fanny was resting at our home, when a lady called and asked to see Miss Crosby, the great hymn-writer. This visitor remained fully two hours. When she went away I joined Aunt Fanny, who said, "Sit down. I have a wonderful story to tell you. That lady was born in the same town as Frances Ridley Havergal, in England, and knew her very well. I recited for her some of the lines that were sent me by the English poetess:

"'Dear blind sister over the sea,
An English heart goes forth to thee.
We are linked by a cable of faith and song,
Flashing bright sympathy swift along;
One in the East and one in the West,
Singing for Him whom our souls love best.'

"My visitor told me she did not come to see me for herself alone, but to tell me the story of her dear boy Will, who went home to God two years ago. 'He was a sweet church chorister,' she said, 'became ill, was taken to the hospital and in two weeks returned—a hopeless case. He loved your hymns and was constantly singing them in the hospital, and several of the patients confessed Christ through his singing "Blessed Assurance." He always had a Moody and Sankey book by his bedside. The evening on which he died was one of those charming English twilights. Will had felt better all day and the doctor encouraged us. I was alone in the house, when I heard the sound of his cane on the floor. On reaching his bedside he said, "Mother, dear, don't leave me. Give me my hymn-book. I want to sing, 'Safe in the arms of Jesus.'" When he reached the line "Hark 'tis the voice of angels," my dear boy dropped the book and his face was illumined as he said. "Ma, there are the angels. There are the fields of glory. There is the jasper sea." And then he passed out to be with them and his Lord forevermore.' "

At an evening service of that day Aunt Fanny told many stories of her hymn-writing which made a deep impression upon her audience. " One of these," she said, " was sent me from a newspaper. I have also heard Mr. Sankey tell the story. 'The congregation of Christ Protestant Episcopal Church, Union Avenue, Allegheny, was startled yesterday by a sensational supplement to the morning service. The church was well filled, and devout worshippers responded to the service as read by the rector, Dr. Robert Meech. The reading had been concluded, and the rector was about to make the usual announcements of future services when an incident occurred such as old Christ Church had never dreamed of. Out of the usual line in a church of this denomination, it was nevertheless marked in its effect, and will never be forgotten by those present.

"'In the fourth pew from the front aisle of the church sat a neatly-dressed woman of intellectual face, apparently about thirty years of age. Her presence as a stranger had been noticed by many, and her deep, tearful interest in the service had been quietly commented on by those who occupied the adjoining pews. At the point mentioned she rose to her feet, and, struggling with emotion, began to speak. The startled congregation was all attention, and she was allowed to proceed. Rapidly and eloquently she told of her going out from the church and of her return to it. In graphic words she painted the hideousness of sin and the joys of a pure life, and as she spoke men and women either gave way to their emotions or listened breathlessly.

"'"I was christened in this church,"

she said, "and attended Sunday-school in the basement when Dr. Paige was rector. My mother was a devout member here, and taught me the right way. At the age of fifteen I deserted my home and married an actor. For a number of years I followed the stage as a profession, leading such a life as naturally accompanies it. In dramatic circles, in variety business, and in the circus, I spent those godless years.

"'"About two years ago I was in the city of Chicago. One afternoon I was on my way to Ferris Wheel Park to spend the afternoon in revelry, when I happened on an open-air meeting which the Epworth League of Grace Methodist Episcopal Church was conducting on North Park Street. I stopped through curiosity, as I believed, to listen; but I know now that God arrested my footsteps there. They were singing 'Saved by Grace,' and the melody impressed me. Recollections of childhood days came trooping into my soul, and I remembered that in all the years of my absence my mother, until her death nine years ago, had been praying for me.

"'"I was converted and, falling on my knees on the curbstone, I asked my Father's pardon. Then and there I received it, and I left the place with a peace which has never forsaken me. I gave up my profession at once and have lived for His service ever since. I have been but a few days in this city. Last night I visited the Hope Mission, and the Lord told me I must come here and testify of what He has done for me. I have not been in this church for many years, but it seems only yesterday that I left it. I have been sitting in the pew directly opposite the one once occupied by my mother and I feel her presence to-day. I could not resist the impulse to give this testimony. The Lord Himself sent me here."

"'The congregation was profoundly impressed. The rector descended from the chancel and, with tears in his eyes, approached the speaker, bidding her Godspeed. The service went on. At its conclusion many members of the congregation shook hands with the stranger and told of their impressions. A stranger might have imagined himself in a Methodist church, so intense was the feeling. The strange visitor departed with a sense of duty done. All she said was: "I feel that the Lord Jesus and mother have been here."'"

I whispered to Aunt Fanny that there were a number of railroad men in the congregation. She took the hint and addressed them: "The railroad men are 'my boys.' I love every one of them and I must say a word to them ere I close. A great many years ago a very dear friend of mine had charge of a large number of railroad men in New York

City. These men had to work seven days in the week, and it was agreed that the room where they waited for the trolleys should be fixed up, and each Sunday morning a service lasting one hour should be conducted in the interest of the conductors and drivers. Here in this dingy little room made cheerful with a bit of red carpet and a few flowers and plants, I began my work with the railroad boys. Many and many a time I have spoken for them in their Y. M. C. A. meetings and in their missions, and it has always cheered my heart when I have heard those strong men sing some of the hymns I have written."

When we returned home that night Aunt Fanny related many instances similar to those set down in this chapter of how her hymns and gospel songs have been blessed to the hearts of men and women the wide world over.

"God has given me a wonderful work

to do," she said, "a work that has brought me untold blessing and great joy. When word is brought to me, as it is from time to time, of some wandering soul being brought back home through one of my hymns, my heart thrills with joy, and I give thanks to God for giving me a share in the glorious work of saving human souls."

VIII

My Teachers and Teaching

All the way my Saviour leads me:
  What have I to ask beside?
Can I doubt His tender mercy
  Who through life has been my guide?
Heavenly faith, divinest comfort
  There by faith in Him to dwell!
For I know whate'er befall me,
  Jesus doeth all things well.

All the way my Saviour leads me,
  Cheers each winding path I tread;
Gives me grace for every trial,
  Feeds me with the living bread;
Though my weary steps may falter,
  And my soul athirst may be,
Gushing from the Rock before me,
  Lo, a spring of joy I see.

All the way my Saviour leads me;
  Oh, the fullness of His love!
Perfect rest to me is promised
  In my Father's house above;
When my spirit, clothed, immortal,
  Wings its flight to endless day,
This my song through endless ages—
  Jesus led me all the way.

[*1874*]

VIII

MY TEACHERS AND TEACHING

"If you devote your time to study you will avoid the irksomeness of life; nor will you long for the approach of night, being tired of day; nor will you be a burden to yourself, nor your society unsupportable to others."

"I HAVE been interested in schools, teachers and teaching all of my life," said Aunt Fanny. "A teacher can easily inspire or depress a pupil. When I was a student some of my teachers did not understand me, and thereby were quite unable to give me what I needed." It was the close of a bright summer day. Aunt Fanny had been visiting the Seminary which has been located in our town along the banks of the Muskonetcong for fifty years. When she returned, she began to talk of her educational life. "My mother, grandmother and a dear old Quaker friend were among my first instructors," she continued. "I was eager for an education. I prayed daily to God that He would open the way for me to get with those who were able to instruct me in the higher branches of learning. When my mother told me that I was to enter the Institution for the Blind in New York City, I clapped my hands and said, 'Thank God, He has answered my prayer.' While I loved my home and mother, I was ready and willing to go away in order to be educated. On the 3d of March, 1835, I came to Norwalk by stage, and then by boat to New York City. A few days were spent with my friends, after which they took me to the Institution. That night I went to my bed with a heavy heart. At breakfast next morning Superintendent Russ came to me and in the kindest way cheered my drooping heart by instructing me in the Scriptures and reading to me some poems.

"I soon felt at home, and was delighted to hear my teachers read the best poetry. There were both boys and girls in the Institution, and some of the teachers were distrustful of them. I said to one of those watch-dog teachers one day: 'Trust the boys and girls, and they won't deceive you. All the pupils hate a tattle tale teacher.'

"There were certain studies that I truly loved. I was wrapped up in them. But I hated mathematics. I had no faculty for it, and the teachers excused me. They were wise in this, for it was not a bit of use seeking to force arithmetic on me. Once I was both helped and hurt by my teacher, who requested to see me at his office. I was elated, thinking he was to commend my work, but to my surprise he talked out of his heart to me concerning people who were flattering my poetry, and warned me with the words: 'A flattering mouth worketh ruin.' I had been thinking that I was a real poetess, but this kind man showed me wherein my work was weak. I was hurt, but I was also helped. After thanking him, I said, 'You have been as a father to me.' From this lesson I learned the best method of dealing with pupils in after days. If I desired to do the most for them, it was best achieved by never correcting them in the presence of others.

"As a pupil and instructor I remained in this Institution for twenty-three years. I was schooled in the best there was in music, art, and literature. When I began to teach, my mind was clearly made up what not to do, so I became a favourite with my pupils. I considered their gifts, and sought to bring out the best that they were capable of doing. For ninety-three years I have kept up with the growth of our school life, and have my personal opinions concerning teaching and teachers. My own view is that much of our public school work to-day is too shallow. The pupils are required to go over so many things that many of them are incompetent to do one thing well. A young man from a high school came to spend an evening with me some time since, and I asked him to read Kipling's 'Recessional.' When he came to the words:

> " 'For heathen heart that puts its trust
> In reeking tube and iron shard,'

he was truly confused. Our high school pupils ought at least to be able to read correctly. In the days when I was a girl we mastered thoroughly one subject. I was able to recite the grammar from beginning to end. I feel our great need is to train teachers not to get merely so much money, and fill in so many hours a year, but to develop in the young American thoroughness and personality.

"Have you studied the life of Helen Keller?" I told her I had. Also that I had spent an hour with her, had read all her books, and had talked with her teacher. When she knew this, Aunt Fanny was willing to stay up all night to hear of my experience with Miss Keller. I brought her the books Helen Keller had written, and placed them in her lap. As she took up one by one, "The Story of My Life," "The World I Live In," "Out of the Dark," and a little volume on "Optimism," Aunt Fanny exclaimed, "Is it possible that one with so many drawbacks has done so much? She puts us all to shame. Truly her teacher is a genius in industry."

The Seminary clock struck twelve as I read from the essay on "Optimism." When I came to the passage, "I am a citizen of the world, I see a brighter spiritual era . . . in which there shall be no England, no France, no Germany no America, but one family, the human race ; one law, peace ; one need, harmony ; one means, labour ; one taskmaster, God," Aunt Fanny sprang from her seat, clapped her hands, and said : " Wonderful vision. She is a Deborah.

"I met her first years ago, and have an engagement to be with her in New York City in the coming fall. In my quiet hours I feel the influence of her teacher-spirit. She is one of the greatest gifts to this age. The way in which the apparently impossible has been achieved in her case is wonderful to think of. Shut up in the dark from all the beautiful things other people depend so much upon for the pleasures of life, she has managed not only to keep happy but to fling sunshine all about her and to bless others in an exceptional and beautiful way. Hers is a splendid triumph over adversity—the triumph of a victorious spirit."

Aunt Fanny took Helen Keller's four volumes with her to her bedroom that night and the next morning recited to me these lines:

There is a chain that links my soul to thine,
I may not clasp thy gentle hand in mine,
And yet in thought each other we may meet,
And spend this day in converse pure and sweet.

I met thee once. 'Twas many years ago,
And yet its memories like a fountain flow;
I hear thy voice, as then its tones I heard,
And fond affection clings to every word.

God keep thee still beneath His watching care,
And strew thy path with buds and blossoms rare,
When other hearts their tribute bring to thee,
Oh, may I ask that mine received may be.

IX

My Notable Preachers

Blessed day when pure devotions
 Rise to God on wings of love;
When we catch the distant music
 Of the angel choirs above.

Blessed day, when bells are calling
 Weary souls from earthly care,
And we come, with hearts uplifted,
 To the holy place of prayer.

Blessed day, so calm and restful,
 Bringing joy and peace to all,
Linger yet in tranquil beauty,
 Ere the shades of evening fall.

Blessed day, thy light is fading;
 One by one its beams depart;
May their calm and sweet reflection
 Still abide in every heart.

[*1894*]

IX

MY NOTABLE PREACHERS

"The best preacher is the heart:
The best teacher is time;
The best book is the world:
The best friend is God."

"TO tell you of all the notable preachers I have known would fill a great volume," said Aunt Fanny. We were travelling together from Bridgeport, Conn., to Amboy, New Jersey. I had gone to the New England town to bring Aunt Fanny to my home, and during the journey I asked her for some impressions of the great men of the pulpit which during her long life she had been privileged both to hear and meet.

"In Bridgeport I have heard some of the ablest men this country has produced," she said. "About twenty-six years ago Randolph S. Foster, Bishop of the Methodist Episcopal Church, preached one of the most masterly sermons that I have ever heard from the text: 'When I consider Thy heavens, the work of Thy fingers, the moon and the stars which Thou hast ordained; What is man that Thou art mindful of him? and the son of man that Thou visitest him?' If there is a third heaven I was there that Sunday morning while listening to that saintly man. He was small of stature, but of a wonderful mind. I heard him several times after that, but to me he never equalled that occasion. I shall bear the message with me into eternity.

"On another occasion I heard Dr. J. O. Peck in the same church. His speech impressed me with the thought that he was truly a master workman. He had a body like Washington, and a voice like a trumpet. There is one story he told

I shall never forget. He was showing the value of individual Christian stewardship, and said, 'There was once a man who made a profession of the Christian religion to whom his pastor sought to show the value of benevolence to his own life. But he replied, "The dying thief was converted and went direct to heaven, and *he* never gave anything towards the heathen nor the expenses of the church." Then the minister asked him if he would permit him to distinguish between him and the dying thief. The poor fellow gave his consent and the minister said, "The man on the cross was a dying thief, but you are a living thief!"'"

Aunt Fanny's voice rang with laughter as she told this story.

"I think *I* have a story as good as that on Christian giving," she said. "I always believe in and carry out in my life the command which runs, 'Honour the Lord with thy substance and first fruits of thy increase, so shall thy barns be filled with plenty and thy presses shall burst out new wine.' A young minister friend of mine once went up to a quiet New England town to spend his vacation with his little boy. The father had given close attention to the training of his only son. They were really companions. The mother had been taken to the Better Land when the boy was born. The preacher had not been in town a week before a deacon of the church came and requested him to preach on Sunday morning, as the man engaged had disappointed them. After some talk with the farmer-deacon the minister consented. It was a lovely Sunday as the preacher and his son wound 'round the 'Pine Path.' He preached a sermon that had in it the idea of race improvement. The people listened well. The service ended without an offering being taken, and it had been the custom of this minister never to appear in the sanctuary without bringing an offering to the Lord. So as he left the church he placed a fifty-cent piece in the box by the door and went down the winding 'Pine Path.' In a few seconds he heard a voice and turning he saw the deacon hastening towards him, who placed in his hand a fifty-cent piece, saying, 'It is our custom up here to present the preacher with whatever we find in the offering boxes for his services.' Then the minister's little boy looked up into his father's face and said, 'Papa, if you had given more you would have gotten more, wouldn't you?'"

We had now reached Stamford and as Fanny heard the name of the town she said, "I remember well the time when Dr. James M. Buckley, that statesman of Methodism, stood for righteousness like a bulwark in this city. Often have I heard him in Brooklyn with pleasure and profit and to-day I love to hear read what he writes. Chaplain McCabe was a live coal from heaven. His singing thrilled my soul. I think he has influenced more people by his songs than any minister of his day. It has been my pleasure often to converse with him and to receive his counsel.

"Bishop Thomas Bowman (who I think was born in the same year as myself) was truly an apostle of power. Bishop Edward Andrews was a statesman worthy of his position. I regard him as one of the sanest and safest Christian gentlemen I have ever known. Sometimes it took quite a while for him to get going, but he always gave you something worth listening to. John P. Newman charmed my soul with his oratorical flights. John Fletcher Hurst has made for himself a great name in the church of which he was a bishop. He was a scholar and a cultured Christian gentleman. I consider him the first writer in Methodism on church history. Bishop Brooks I revered. He was the big man of the Episcopalian Church. The greatest lecture it has been my privilege to hear was one delivered by Bishop Charles H. Fowler on Lincoln. It is beyond my powers of description."

As we entered New York City Aunt Fanny remarked, "Here and in Brooklyn I have heard some mighty men." We went down to the Jersey ferry in a hack, and as we crossed the North River she said, "All the big men that we have been talking about to-day rise before me like a dream. I have a whole garden full of them in my mind. Matthew Simpson I shall never forget. He showed me the beauties of the world that now is, and of that which is to come. Henry Ward Beecher, whom I knew well, was the greatest of pulpit orators of the nineteenth century, if not of any century. When I lived in Brooklyn he was bitterly persecuted, but like the Hebrew children he came out of the flames unhurt. Dr. Richard Salter Storrs, one year younger than myself, was a man of lofty principles and purity of motive. His influence in the city was salient. Dr. John Hall of the Fifth Avenue Presbyterian Church in New York was a dear friend of mine. His sermons were rich in thought and helpful in spirit. Dr. Howard Crosby was a scholarly preacher. I never went to hear him without feeling I was richly repaid.

"Two ministers, who lived in Brooklyn during my residence there, bore names precious to me—Dr. Behrends and Dr. Cuyler. Dr. Behrends, of the Central Congregational Church, was a safe man in the pulpit and out of it. He built firmly on the foundation of God which standeth sure. But the great pastor was Theodore L. Cuyler. For thirty years he was a most successful pastor of the Lafayette Avenue Presbyterian Church, and I highly value his books, 'God's Light On Dark Clouds,' 'Christianity In the Home,' and 'How to Be a Pastor.' Though not as eloquent as some Brooklyn divines, none were more respected or useful than Dr. Cuyler. If you desire to be a prince among pastors read and follow Theodore L. Cuyler."

The ferry-boat entered the slip with a bang. "Be careful, Captain," said Aunt Fanny, "you have precious freight aboard." Our hackman listened to his passenger with close attention, and when I informed him that she was Fanny Crosby, who had written "Safe in the Arms of Jesus," he took off his hat and wept. He called a policeman and said, "This is Miss Fanny Crosby, who wrote 'Safe in the Arms of Jesus.' I want you to help this young man to get her safely to the train."

"I sure will," said the policeman. Then quite sadly he added, "We sang that hymn at my little girl's funeral last week."

Aunt Fanny took the policeman's arm and said, "I call all the policemen and railroad men 'my boys.' They take such good care of me wherever I go." The officer assisted her with greatest care and as she took her seat in the train she said to him, "God bless your dear heart. You shall have my prayers. Tell your dear wife that your little daughter is safe in the arms of Jesus." The great strong policeman turned away wiping the tears from his eyes.

For half an hour after the train pulled out of the station Aunt Fanny was silent as if asleep. Then she roused herself and said, "I have been thinking about you. You are a young minister of God. The notables of whom I have spoken have brought much sunshine into my life. Live close to their example and you will not live in vain. The mission of a minister is matchless. You never have to apologize for your message. Be careful and guard against fads, cranks and schisms; for these have done more real harm to the growth of the Kingdom of God among men than anything else I have known. Once a man came into a meeting at which I was present and after having listened to a stirring address on foreign missions stood up and said with a nasal whine: 'Talk about foreign missions! Why, there is plenty of work to do at home. Go down on the streets of our city and see our boys and young men. Go to church and see forty bonnets to one bald pate. It's time, brothers and sisters, that we went to work at home; and if you don't look out, brothers and sisters, there will not be men enough in heaven to sing bass.' "

By this time the train had reached Amboy. I took Aunt Fanny down along the

"Bluff" in an auto where she could catch a whiff of sea breeze, hear the splash of the waves, look out towards the open sea and feel upon her face the glow of the sunset that was kissing the billows into golden splendour away out towards Sandy Hook. Such an experience she specially enjoyed. She seemed always to be communing with the tumbling waters, and to be answering in her heart little Paul Dombey's question: "What are the wild waves saying?" To Fanny Crosby they were ever telling of God's goodness, of a Heavenly Father's care.

X

Making the Best of Everything

Sing with a tuneful spirit,
  Sing with a cheerful lay,
Praise to thy great Creator,
  While on the pilgrim way.
Sing when the birds are waking,
  Sing with the morning light;
Sing in the noontide's golden beam,
  Sing in the hush of night.

Sing when the heart is troubled,
  Sing when the hours are long,
Sing when the storm-cloud gathers;
  Sweet is the voice of song.
Sing when the sky is darkest,
  Sing when the thunders roll;
Sing of the land where rest remains,
  Rest for the weary soul.

Sing in the vale of shadows,
  Sing in the hour of death,
And, when the eyes are closing,
  Sing with the latest breath.
Sing till the heart's deep longings
  Cease on the other shore;
Then, with the countless numbers there
  Sing on forevermore.

[*1869*]

X

MAKING THE BEST OF EVERYTHING

> " O joy that seekest me through pain,
> I cannot close my heart to thee;
> I trace the rainbow through the rain,
> And feel the promise is not vain
> That morn shall tearless be."

"WELL, it might have been worse," said Aunt Fanny. "No one was drowned. I have long since learned that 'what can't be cured must be endured.' Some days are good, some days are ill. But it never pays to murmur, and it is useless to worry."

It was the morning after a severe storm. Before bedtime, the night before, the winds had begun to howl and the incoming tide played havoc with the docks, bridges and boats. At daybreak it looked as if a great, cruel hand had been tearing things to shivers. I described the wake of the storm to Aunt Fanny, and this was her reply.

"Yes," she went on, "years ago I made up my mind to make the best of everything. I was brought to this decision by hearing my old friend, Dr. Deems, recite:

"'Dear friend,
The world is wide
In time and tide
And God is guide;
Then do not hurry.
That man is blest
Who does his best
And leaves the rest;
Then do not worry.'

"In my quiet moments I say to myself, 'Fanny, there are many worse things than blindness that might have happened to you. The loss of the mind is a thousand times worse than the loss of the eyes.' Then I might have been speechless and deaf. I do not know, but on the whole it has been a good thing that I *have* been blind. How in the world could I have lived such a helpful life as I have lived had I not been blind? I am very well satisfied. I never let anything trouble me, and to my implicit faith, and to my implicit trust in my heavenly Father's goodness, I attribute my good health and long life. If I didn't get the thing I wanted one day, well, I'd usually get it the next. If not then, well, I realized that it wasn't good for me to have it at all. In the case of my loss of sight I can see how the Lord permitted it. He didn't order it; He permitted it. I have heard my heavenly Father say: 'What I do thou knowest not now, but thou shalt know hereafter,' and for my consolation I repeat:

"'His purposes will ripen fast,
Unfolding every hour;
The bud may have a bitter taste,
But sweet will be the flower.'

"During my long life I have had many a hard struggle, with bread to provide and rent to pay, but I never lost faith in the promise, 'Thy bread shall be given, and thy water sure.' My constant petition was, 'Give me neither poverty nor riches.' This prayer has been answered, and for the past sixteen years my old publishers, The Biglow & Main Co. have, in consideration of my many years of association with them, granted me a regular allowance.

"Here we are to-day; the rain is pouring down, the wind is whistling, the day is chilly, yet I am as happy as a lark. He who takes care of the sparrow will never forget Aunt Fanny. 'To-morrow the sun will be shining, although it is gloomy to-day.' It's worth a thousand dollars a year to look on the bright side of things. Many a storm has beaten on this old bark of mine, but I always enter the harbour singing:

"'God moves in a mysterious way
His wonders to perform,
He plants His footsteps on the sea
And rides upon the storm.

* * * * *

"'Blind unbelief is sure to err,
And scan His works in vain.
God is His own interpreter,
And He will make it plain.'

"I carefully studied history, philosophy and science," Aunt Fanny continued, "and was often perplexed about sin in the world. For a long time it was a problem I was unable to solve. I thought about it, dreamed about it, and saw no use for it. Finally I reached the conclusion that this was the best world order that could be conceived, and that if people were in the world without anything to contend with, they would speedily become pygmies. So I stopped troubling about it, and made every endeavour to conquer and make the best of it.

"The sufferings of life caused me no

little anxiety. Just as last night's storm banged the boats, the wharfs, and the nets, so sickness comes, and tears things apart. While thinking over this I was consoled by reading, 'He whom thou lovest is sick.' Then I said, 'Suffering is no argument of God's displeasure.' It is a part of the fibre of our lives. So I settled that question and made the best of it.

"When sorrows came to myself and to my friends, it almost made my heart bleed, and I asked myself why I should go thus sorrowing? In looking a little deeper I found sorrow to be one of the threads in the skein of life that must be woven in the warp and woof of existence, and that the things that were too wonderful for me to fathom I must leave in the hands of Him who is able to sustain under all circumstances. It was while thinking along these lines that I also thought of some lines I wrote away back in the seventies:

Fast Friends for Fifty Years:
Fanny J. Crosby and Hubert P. Main

Never be sad or desponding,
If thou hast faith to believe;
Grace for the duties before thee,
Ask of thy God and receive.
Never be sad or desponding,
There is a morrow for thee,
Soon thou shalt dwell in the brightness,
There with the Lord thou shalt be.

"Half a lifetime has passed since I wrote those lines, and a thousand and one experiences have been mine in the years that lie between. But nothing has happened or threatened which could have warranted my altering a single syllable or thought they contain. In sunshine and shadow, in sickness and in health, through every step of the journey, God has given grace and glory. There is nothing surprising in this. It is according to His promise, 'And no good thing will He withhold from them that walk uprightly.' This I have always tried to do, my Saviour helping me, and God has looked after the fulfillment of His part of the promise. For me, life has been short of many things that some people would probably rather die than be without. That is their misfortune—not mine. It is not the things I've missed, or never had, which make me sorrowful. It is the things I have *had* in full measure in which I rejoice daily. That's how I feel to-day, and it was in the same spirit that I wrote the lines which have been proved abundantly true in my own life and work:

> God will take care of you, be not afraid,
> He is your safeguard through sunshine and
> shade;
> Tenderly watching, and keeping His own,
> He will not leave you to wander alone."

XI

My Love For Children

They are buds of hope and promise
  Blessed by Him whose Name is Love;
Lent us here to train and nourish
  For a better life above;
Tender plants by angels guarded,
  Clinging vines the children are;
Jewels in our hearts to glisten,
  Precious treasures, O how fair!

* * * * *

I have heard the children singing
  When my heart was lone and sad;
I have heard them in the distance
  And their music made me glad.
But their voices cheer and charm me
  In the Sabbath homes they love;
And I think they will be sweetest
  In the saintly choirs above.

XI

MY LOVE FOR CHILDREN

> "Ah, what would the world be to us
> If the children were no more?
> We should dread the desert behind us
> Worse than the dark before."

"PLEASE, Aunt Fanny, will you tell us a story?"

We were gathered under an old apple tree in the merry month of June. A children's party had been arranged for the blind singer and a dozen children were sitting around her. She was a true child among them. Together they played games, recited pieces and sang many of Fanny's hymns. Then one of the youngsters asked her for a story. "Bless your dear heart," she replied. "Of course I will. I have lots of them stored away for children." Then she began: "A certain man had two children, a boy and girl. The lad was a handsome young fellow enough, but the girl was as plain as a girl could be, and, provoked beyond endurance by the way her brother looked in the glass and made remarks to her disadvantage, she went to her father and complained of it. The father drew his children to him very tenderly. 'My dears,' he said, 'I wish you both to look in the glass every day. You, my son, so that, seeing your face is handsome, may take care not to spoil it by ill-temper and bad behaviour; and you, my daughter, that you may be encouraged to make up for your want of beauty by the sweetness of your manners and the grace of your conversation.'"

The children looked gravely at each other, and then one said, "Tell us another, Aunt Fanny." She smiled as she drew a little book of four pages from her bag. Turning the first page towards the children she asked them its colour. They all shouted, "Black."

"Well," said Aunt Fanny, "that represents sin. I want you to remember that sin ruins the sinner. Sin is always black. It is the transgression of the law. What is this colour?"

"Red," was the ready reply.

"Yes, red. And red is for blood, and I want you ever to remember that you are redeemed by the precious blood of Christ. 'Unto Him who hath loved us and hath washed us from our sins in His own blood, unto Him be honour and praise forever.' The next page, you see, is white. That is for right. Dare to do right. Dare to be true. You have heard the verse which runs:

> "'Dare to be a Daniel,
> Dare to stand alone,
> Dare to have a purpose firm
> And dare to make it known.'

The last page is gold. It stands for glory. He will give you grace and glory, all along your pilgrim way. Then this golden colour represents the celestial city, with its streets of pure gold." Here she paused and bowed her head for a moment. Then she went on: "Dear children, I had a little sister once with whom I loved to play, but God's good angel came down and took her to our Father's heavenly home and when she went I wrote these lines:

She's gone, ah, yes, her lovely form
Too soon has ceased to bloom,
An emblem of a fragile flower,
That blossoms for the tomb.
She's gone, yet why should we repine,
Our darling is at rest;
Her cherub spirit now reclines
Upon her Saviour's breast."

Aunt Fanny drank her cup of tea with the children and then she said, "Before we go I will recite you some verses of a poem of mine, written after a person had

"Aunt Fanny" Among the Children

asked me if I loved children. I love you, dear children, with all my heart and soul, and would rather be driven out from among men than to be disliked by children:

Love the children? What a question!
  Cold indeed the heart must be
That can turn without emotion
  From their laughter gushing free.
Yes, with all my heart I love them;
  Bless the children every one!
I can be a child among them,
  And enjoy their freaks and fun.

* * * *

Love the children? I can never,
  Never pass them in the street,
But my every pulse awaking,
  Thrills with love to all I meet;
I have heard the children singing
  When my heart was lone and sad,
I have heard them in the distance,
  And their music makes me glad."

The children clung around Aunt Fanny as she entered the house, there to be greeted by the parents of the children at a reception given in her honour.

"My dear friends," she said, "I am so happy to greet you to-day. I have had a lovely time with your children, and I want now to recite some lines I have specially written for this occasion:

Among the honoured guests to-day,
Within this home, I'd gladly stay.
I come, your many friends to see
And take a social cup of tea.

Your floral plan is just the thing,
With eager joy its praises ring,
And well they may, for too we trace
Your handiwork in every place.

Your dining-room arrayed with care,
The summer daisies blooming there,
Sweet daisies from the meadow green
That add new beauty to the scene.

But hark! my signal calls away.
I would but cannot longer stay.
Beloved friends and patrons all
I hope you'll soon return my call.
Your daisy chain, your cup of tea
Will in my heart remembered be."

XII

American Hearts and Homes

* * * * *

Though dreary and wild was that wave-girt shore,
And cold was the wintry air,
The voice of the tyrant was heard no more;
The angel of peace was there;
And a radiant gem from her crown she set
In the path where the moonlight roams—
A star that in glory is shining yet
O'er American hearts and homes.

O, that beacon of hope in the darkest hour
That hung o'er oppression's night
Was the guard of the brave; and they felt its power
As they looked on its steady light;
But o'er each link of the tyrant's chain
The surge of old ocean foams,
And Freedom the goddess that dwells and reigns
In American hearts and homes.

* * * * *

Let me die in the land where my native streams
In their stately grandeur flow;
Where the tender smile of affection beams,
And the skies in their beauty glow;
On the standard of Freedom my eyes would rest
Ere my spirit heavenward roams;
I would give the last sigh of a faithful breast
For American hearts and homes.

XII

AMERICAN HEARTS AND HOMES

"On the standard of Freedom my eyes would rest
Ere my spirit heavenward roams;
I would give the last sigh of a faithful breast
To American hearts and homes."

"FOR eighty years I have watched the growth of the American home," said Aunt Fanny, "and there is nothing than concerns me more than the homes of our dear home land." We were in the cupola of our house, Fanny and I, where I had taken her after a good night's rest. It was shielded from the wind by a sea-view window, and I told her of the old church, built in Queen Anne's day, that could be seen from where we sat and which bore the marks of the Revolutionary guns. I told her also of the Governor's mansion, where Benjamin

Franklin remained overnight, and of the old families and homes of the town that was four days older than New York.

"I have a poem, 'American Hearts and Homes,'" said Aunt Fanny. "And I believe that no nation can rise above the level of its home life. In reading the spirit of the age I am somewhat afraid that we are breaking certain ties and permitting certain fires in the home life to die out which is a menace to our national life. Fine furniture, buildings and books alone never make a real permanent home. There must be the communion of souls. My home life was such that my days were guarded wheresoever I was. I was taught love, loyalty and reverence for my nation and all things good and true. I know it sounds fine to shout for the flag as the standard of our country, but to stand firmly by it in the time of danger is wiser."

"Aunt Fanny," I said, "do you think

that the home life of to-day is changed from that which obtained when you were growing up?"

"For many years I have watched the trend of the people," she answered, "and I really do think that the home ties do not bind as strongly as in my girlhood. Many attractions that were quite unknown in my early days are found in every city to-day. Clubs and society take up so much of a mother's spare time nowadays that there seems scarcely a moment in which to do the work that ought to be done in the home. It may appear a little old-fogeyish but I have firm convictions on this very vital question.

"It is essential that both in home and state we should know the law of cause and effect. To turn a boat lose on yonder sound to the mercy of wind and tide would, we know, result in a ruined craft. And just as a boat needs a guiding hand, so the nation and the home needs some one at the helm or the winds and waves of the world will work havoc and disaster."

"What do you think are the safest methods to adopt for home and country improvement?"

Aunt Fanny raised her head as if looking towards the sea and said, "A few nights ago I sat thinking over a better nation through a better home. The better the soil the richer the crop. The stronger the home the safer the state. I said to myself, 'Fanny, if this home and nation is to endure it must be peaceful. Peace and harmony are the prominent, polished pillars of every home and nation. Discord has blighted more firesides and crushed more nations than any other internal foe. The price of peace must be paid, or the solid marble pillar will bend. Prosperity is the goodly child of peace.'"

Aunt Fanny paused and taking a little New Testament from her bag continued.

"When I was a child this book had a practical place in both home and nation. During these many years my love for the Holy Bible has not waned. Its truth was not only born with me; it was bred into my life. My mother and grandmother took pains that I knew the Bible better than any other book. All that I am and all that I ever expect to be in literature or life is due to the Bible. Well do I remember learning that hymn of Charles Wesley:

"'When quiet in my house I sit,
 Thy book be my companion still;
My joy Thy sayings to repeat,
 Talk o'er the record of Thy will,
And search the oracles divine,
Till every heartfelt word is mine.'"

I had just returned from the Burns country and told her of the cottage in which Scotland's greatest songster was born. I talked to her of Ayr, of Alloway Kirk and Dumfries. Then I read several of Burns' poems, finishing with "The Cotter's Saturday Night." This she requested me to read again. When I reached the line, "The priest-like father reads the sacred page," "That's what I mean," she broke in with, "the Book must be read by the father in the home. A Scotchman once told me that his country was greatly enriched from the use of the Scripture around the fireside. No Christian nation can be great which ignores the Sacred Book. Read me those lines, commencing 'Then kneeling down ——' over again," and her face gleamed as I did so.

"Then kneeling down to heaven's eternal King,
  The saint, the father, and the husband prays.
Hope springs exulting on triumphant wing,
  That thus they all shall meet in future days,
There ever bask in uncreated rays."

"I find in that verse," said Aunt Fanny, "the strength of the nation and the home; and I know that homes cannot exist long as permament places in uplifting the nation if heads of the families are prayerless. Neither can the nation rise to its highest with prayerless Presidents. Our greatest Presidents have been men with unfaltering faith in prayer. The spirit in 'The Cotter's Saturday Night' must be carried out. 'They round the ingle, form a circle wide.' The people of the United States must know if the home fails the Church is shorn of its strength, the community crumbles, the State is unstable, the nation doomed. I am an optimist, who through the light sees the danger point. If I could direct the reading of the home, I'd save the State. If I could select the friends that frequent the home, I would secure its future. If I could bring the unseen Guest into the home and nation as suggested by Dean Alford, I should be happy. Nothing of education or culture or breeding can take the place of Christ in the home—of Jesus in the heart. His presence alone can prevent selfishness having dominion; and where selfishness is true happiness can never be found. But with the influence of the Master dominant, all is well.

> "My bark is wafted to the strand,
> By breath divine,
> And on the helm there rests a hand
> Other than mine.
>
> "One who was known in storms to sail,
> I have on board;
> Above the roaring of the gale
> I hear my Lord."

Just then the whistles blew, and the dinner bell rang. As we went down to dine I felt I had been looking out of the sea-view window with one of the great women of our time.

XIII

My Visit to Cambridge

Cool from the wells of Elim,
Softly the waters bright
Under the waving palm-trees
Smiled in the peaceful light;
There were the tents so goodly,
There was a nation strong,
Resting awhile by Elim's wells,
Praising the Lord in song.

* * * *

Out of the rock from Horeb,
Smote by a wondrous rod,
Quickly the gushing waters
Came at the voice of God;
They who athirst were pining
They who rebelled before,
Now with delight and wonder filled,
Drank, and were glad once more

Purer than wells of Elim,
Under the palm-trees fair,
Sweeter than Horeb's waters
Hailed by the fainting there—
Lo, at the feet of mercy
Fresh from the springs above,
Jesus the living water gives,
Bought with redeeming love.

[*1883*]

XIII

MY VISIT TO CAMBRIDGE

"I HAVE had the time of my life," said Aunt Fanny as she entered our home one day. She clapped her hands and continued, "I have been to Harvard, and everybody seemed to do everything they were able to do to make my stay there most delightful.

"Just think. I am ninety-two years of age and have been sitting at the feet of the professors of Harvard College. I feel like a girl again. Truly I have drunk from the crystal streams of thought and knowledge.

"Why should one cease to learn because old age is creeping in upon him? I am learning something new every day of my life. The wide world is my schoolroom. All nature is my teacher, 'and never too old to learn' my motto.

"I suppose you are curious to know how I happened to visit Cambridge. Well, over thirty years ago I met a young Baptist preacher who was very much concerned in my work among the railroad men and among the outcast. His name was Campbell. He was a sturdy Scotch Canadian. I felt that he had in him great possibilities, and soon he was called to a large church in this educational centre. You know a clergyman must continue to climb if he is to hold his own in the shadow of old Harvard. This he has done. For years I had lost sight of him, but now through some dear friends the door was thrown wide open for my visit. It had always been one of the great desires of my heart to visit Harvard and come if only for a brief space under the influence of that haunt of literary and educational power.

"A drizzling cold rain, which would have chilled many at my age, was falling but that did not discourage me in the least. We started with a song, 'What care I for time or tide.' On the way to Boston I had four hours of the sweetest expectation possible. On reaching Back Bay Station, a taxi met us and the good Scotch minister took me up in his arms and landed me safely in a cushion seat, and before I could say 'Jack Robinson' I was at 300 Magazine Street, Cambridge.

"Just as the evening meal was over, the door-bell rang, and a delegation from the Salvation Army entered with a request they be permitted to accompany me to the church (where I was to speak) with a brass band and play some of my hymns. This request was readily granted and so the next evening they came with their instruments and played many of my songs in front of the manse. Then followed by hundreds of people I marched from the house to the church, to the music of 'Rescue the Perishing.' They told me that more than two thousand people were present. I spoke to them from my very heart of that wonderful story of Jesus Christ who came into this world with a love big enough to fill every nook and corner of it, if only mankind would allow Him. It was a great service, the presence of Christ being felt both in the music and the message.

"I shall never forget that service to my dying day; and I think I shall remember when I join the Church Triumphant before God and the Lamb. When it was over I slept like a child at the joy of being able in story and in song to tell of my Saviour's boundless love.

"The next night the church was again well filled to hear this little blind woman tell the story of her life. Many of them after the message greeted me and wondered why I was so happy and strong at such a good old age. I told them it was all in the story of that little hymn 'Hide Thou me.'

In thy cleft, O Rock of Ages,
Hide Thou me;
When the fitful tempest rages,
Hide Thou me;
Where no mortal arm can sever
From my heart Thy love forever,
Hide me, O Thou Rock of Ages,
Safe in Thee.

"The next evening the Locus Musical Club gave me a reception. That was as a green pasture in my life. They sang for me until I felt I was raised to the third heaven. I told them some funny stories and did my best to make the evening one of good cheer. They were a lovely lot of people. You know, Boston people can't help being nice. I'm a New Englander myself and love the strength and habits of its people. I felt highly honoured at having such splendid people come to see and entertain me.

"When they told me that many of the professors of Harvard College were to call the next evening I said to myself, 'Now, Fanny Jane, you must put on your best behaviour, and look as wise as Aristotle.' I had heard and read of the great men of Harvard from my girlhood days, and as I have already told you, had always a burning desire to get in some way under the influence of Harvard College.

"My opportunity had now come. I was dressed in my best 'bib and tucker.' I must confess I never met a more cordial company of cultured men in all my life. There was one thing that I carefully noticed, and that was, each professor possessed the gift of a strong hand. You know I judge people largely by the touch of the hand, and I am always cautious when I shake hands with a weak-handed person. What a delight it was to me to be able to sit down by the side of Oliver Clinton Wendell, that master in the science of astronomy. I felt like a child at the feet of a master. He told me more about the heavens in that short time than I had learned in all my life.

"My conversation with the professors was most entertaining. I told them that I had always had a deep interest in Harvard College, as one of my ancestors, Simon Crosby, was one of its founders, and that his son graduated therefrom in 1653. They were all deeply interested in the story of my forebears, and as I told them of my association with the Presidents and many notable men in music, art, and literature, they were much interested. I had to tell them, too, of Princeton, and my visits there to the home of President Cleveland.

"During the evening our conversation

was directed towards many persons and problems of modern life. At last one of them spoke of Mr. Roosevelt, as the peacemaker between Japan and Russia. I have always enjoyed the spirit of 'the Colonel,' and this story was related to me concerning him when a student at Harvard.

"One afternoon he had to declaim. He had an abundance of confidence and was never known to break down in an oration. He marched onto the platform with an air of tenacity, and began in a high key:

> "'At midnight in his lonely tent
> The Turk lay dreaming of the hour,
> When Greece her knee ——'

here he became confused and forgot the next word. He gritted his teeth, closed his eyes and repeated, 'Greece her knee, —Greece her knee,—Greece her knee.' The professor seeing the dilemma of his student looked up with a smile and said,

'Greece her knee again, Theodore, and maybe she'll go.'

"Altogether I was treated so loyally, and entertained so interestingly that I did not want the professors to leave. What a joy it is to associate with such men. The next day they sent me so many flowers and so much fruit that I was compelled to share their generosity with others.

"I went to my room feeling that I had been highly honoured, and that I had a goodly heritage. A certain feeling crept over me that it is difficult to describe. Truly I had found the Wells of Elim and I thought of my own song:

> Cool from the wells of Elim,
> Softly the waters bright,
> Under the waving palm trees,
> Smiled in the peaceful light;
> There were the tents so goodly,
> There was a nation strong,
> Resting awhile by Elim's wells,
> Praising the Lord in song.

"Purer than wells of Elim
  Under the palm trees fair,
Sweeter than Horeb's waters
  Hailed by the fainting there,—
Lo, at the feet of mercy,
  Fresh from the springs above,
Jesus the living water gives,
  Bought with redeeming love.

I sat in my rocking-chair in a musing mood. I did not feel like retiring; it seemed as if all the scenes associated with Harvard's noble past came crowding around me. I sat far into the night in a sort of transported reverie, living over again the stirring scenes of American history and letters which revolve around old Harvard's famous walls."

Here the door-bell rang. It was a call for Aunt Fanny to visit a home in the neighbourhood that had been stricken by the sudden removal of the father of the family. She sprang to her feet, and said, "I must go at once," and away she sped on her mission of comfort.

That night she spoke in my church. "My dear friends," she said, "I know there are hearts in this community that are broken, and souls that are going through Gethsemane. I went to such a family here to-day, and prayed with them in their sorrow, and sought to give a bit of comfort in their distress. We are told in the story of the Israelites' sojourn in the desert of their coming to a place where they found the water so bitter that neither they nor their cattle could drink it. Because of this the encampment was named Marah. For those dear hearts who had come to the bitter waters of life I have written a short poem called 'Marah's Waters':

Not always on the mountain
The sweetest flowers we find,
But sometimes in the valley,
With cypress branches twined
We see their buds unclosing,
Their blossoms bending low,
A hallowed fragrance breathing
Where Marah's waters flow.

O valley of submission,
Where once the Son of God,
Our precious loving Saviour,
In lonely silence trod.
And when our hearts are breaking,
To Him we there may go,
Assured that He is nearest,
Where Marah's waters flow.

O valley of submission,
Where, leaning on His breast,
We tell Him all our sorrow,
And feel the calm of rest.
Tho' oft He gently leads us,
Where verdant pastures grow
His Mercy shines the brightest
Where Marah's waters flow.

"There is one other delightful thought I want to leave with you and that is, that while we have our days of sorrow we also have our seasons of joy. I always look on the bright side of life. I love youth and all that brings sunshine into the home and church. I like birthdays, not so much because my friends send me so many cheery words and tokens of friend-

Fanny Crosby at Seventy-five

ship, but because of the pleasure that I may be able to give to them. I have written hundreds of birthday poems, and I want, by way of closing, to recite one I have written for a very dear friend. It is called 'A Birthday Vision.'

Bending o'er me like a cherub
  At the morning's rosy dawn,
While Aurora's magic fingers
  Robed in light the dewy lawn,
Came a form of rarest beauty
  And these words I heard her say,
Dear Irene, My precious treasure
  Hails her eighteenth year to-day.

When an infant in her cradle,
  I have watched her though unseen,
I have scattered buds and blossoms
  O'er the pathway of Irene,
I was made her guardian angel
  And to me the charge was given,
Still to keep and shield her footsteps
  All the way from earth to heaven.

She is reared by tender parents
  In her home affection dwells,
And the love that clings about her
  Of a perfect union tells;

Give to her a birthday greeting
  Wafted from celestial bowers,
And a garland I have brought her
  From a sunny vale of flowers.

The speaker called her minstrels
  With their hands to crown the scene,
Hope and friendship, joy and music
  Sang the birthday of Irene,
As I gazed in all its splendour
  Burst the glorious orb of day,
And our dear one's guardian angel
  Plumed her wings and soared away.

Dear Irene, My voice repeats it
  While I clasp thy hand in mine,
This the prayer my heart is breathing
  May a cloudless life be thine."

XIV

Ninety Golden Years

* * * * *

Yet a little while we linger
  Ere we reach the journey's end;
Yet a little while of labour,
  Ere the evening shades descend;
Then we'll lay us down to slumber
  But the night will soon be o'er;
In the bright, the bright forever
  We shall slumber never more.

    On the banks beyond the river
      We shall meet no more to sever,
    In the bright, the bright forever,
      In the summer-land of song.

O the bliss of life eternal!
  O the long unbroken rest
In the golden fields of pleasure,
  In the region of the blest!
But to see our dear Redeemer
  And before His throne to fall
There to hear His gracious welcome,
  Will be sweeter far than all.

    On the banks beyond the river
      We shall meet no more to sever
    In the bright, the bright forever,
      In the summer-land of song.

XIV

NINETY GOLDEN YEARS

"Our lives are albums written through
With good or ill, with false or true;
And as the blessed angels turn
The pages of our years,
God grant they read the good with smiles,
And blot the ill with tears!"

"MY dear, dear friends," said Aunt Fanny, "I am happy to greet you here to-night. These ninety years are rich with the wealth of goodness sparkling with the best spirit of sweetness and overflowing with the true wine of joy and gladness."

It was a Sabbath day in October and crowds of people filled the church to hear Aunt Fanny Crosby tell the story of ninety golden years. She stood by a small table that was loaded down with the sunburst roses. As she lovingly caressed the flowers she went on, "I come to you in the evening tide of life with a rod and a staff, and I am living in the sight of eternity's sunrise. Hope's star shines clearer on my pathway to-night than it did fifty years ago. It is the never fading flower of my life, it enriches and beautifies my every hour. Hope has always been the burden of my song. It is, to-night, the dominant factor in my life of industry. It lights my morning hours, it brightens my noon-day activities, it glows in the evening shadows. I constantly am writing of the door of hope for downcast souls and I shall carry on the ministry of hope till I shall enter the Celestial City.

"During these ninety years I have made a careful study of human nature, and I know a person by the touch of the hand or the sound of the voice. Even the footstep is to me a token of the character of its owner. I never feel safe in the company of a person with a very pious, whining voice. I have seldom made a mistake in the selection of my friends during these ninety years. Once in a while I have been fooled by frauds, but not often. Dwight L. Moody once told me something that has often helped me. 'Fanny,' he said, 'be careful whenever you see a man with long hair or a woman with short hair. Usually (though not always) they are freaks; and schism and freaks were ever strong hindrances to the advance of the Christian faith.'

"My love for the beautiful has developed with age. The sunset on the Great Lakes or over the bounding billows has a wonderful charm for me. The fragrance of these beautiful sunburst roses here to-night inspires me to say a word concerning the good, the beautiful, the true. A whiff of the sea-breeze is life giving to my heart. The artist touch in city or country I always enjoy. At

Christmas-time my room must have the holly and the mistletoe, and at Easter I live with the lily and the rose.

"During these ninety years I have been careful of cultivating a sunny disposition, for I have found in my experience so many who when they grow old become bitter and difficult to get along with. I made up my mind, years ago, that I would never become a disagreeable old woman, and that wherever I went I would take sunshine and good cheer. I belong to the Sunshine Society. It is my purpose in old age to grow ripe, and rich, and heavenly. I must be loved rather than feared. Many sorrows which have been heartrending have crossed my path, but out of my Gethsemane I have reached Olivet where angel voices have beckoned me to lands of strength and eternal sunshine. Of malice I can safely say I have none. I love the company of children better to-day than I did fifty years ago. I am at perfect ease in their company. I am happy to know there are so many here to-night. I always say, 'Bring the children. Aunt Fanny has something for the children.'

"I have sought each day to be one of God's unselfish souls. From the time when I received the first check for my poems I made up my mind to open my hand wide to those who needed assistance. During these ninety years I have never served for mere pay. I have always wanted to do a full day's work regardless of what the financial result might be. He who only works for pay gets nothing more. Gold is good in its place, my dear friends, but when it becomes our master, it places a crown of thorns upon the brow that crushes the strongest to the earth. Better a man without money than money without the man.

"My simple trust in God's goodness has never failed me during these many years, since I learned the lesson of 'trust and obey.' The Lord has duly and truly been my Good Shepherd, and has never permitted me to want; for two good angels, Mercy and Truth, have followed me all the days of my life, and I will dwell in the house of the Lord forever. For me to doubt the care of Him who watches the sparrow fall would be a sin. Faith supplies me with good gifts from my Father's hand. My whole life has been an example of the lines:

> " Trust on, as clouds of evening glide away,
> And leave the calm reflection of the day.
> Soon shall thy waiting eyes His glory see,
> And though through clouds it come, so let it be.

" My desire for a long life has been fulfilled. I claimed the promise, 'With long life will I satisfy thee and show thee My salvation.' I wrote a poem to one of my dear friends a little while since which expresses my heart thought in this connection. My mother lived to be ninety-one, and my grandmother to be one hundred and three, so I wrote:

> Firm as a rock since first we met,
> Your love to me has been;
> And this is why I venture now
> To tax it once again.
>
> Please greet the church I hold so dear,
> And to its pastor say,
> The kind remembrance he has shown
> On this my natal day,
>
> I never, never shall forget,
> And if I still survive,
> I hope to greet thee when I reach
> One hundred years and five.

"But if my heavenly Father will it otherwise it is well. I am but waiting by the river's brink, watching for the incoming of the tide. Then I shall, with my Pilot, enter the haven of eternal sunshine and service. My dear friends, I am a great admirer of the poetry of Lord Tennyson, but I do not like one of his lines in the poem 'Crossing the Bar.' He says, 'I hope to see my Pilot face to face, When I have crossed the bar.' Now, *I* would say, 'I *know* I'll see my Pilot face to face, When I have crossed the bar.'

"I know people are very anxious to hear something about the mode of living which has helped me to live so long and so well. From girlhood days to this present hour I have had three little angel-guards. The first angel guards my taste. I am always careful about my eating. There are things that I'd love to eat but the angel-guard says, 'You'd better not.' I follow the simplest form of diet—fresh eggs, fruit, vegetables, spring chicken, and I love a cup of tea. The next angel-guard controls my temper. I early made up my mind that when people lose their tempers they usually make fools of themselves, so I resolved always to keep mine. The next angel-guard is over my tongue and I constantly pray, 'Set a watch, O

Lord, over my mouth, keep Thou the door of my lips.' When quite a girl I learned this message from the Psalm:

> " 'What man is he that desireth life, and loveth many days, that he may see good?
> Keep thy tongue from evil, and thy lips from speaking guile.
> Depart from evil, and do good; seek peace, and pursue it.'

"My methods of work are very simple. I retire to my room about ten o'clock and spend two hours in thinking out a poem, going over every line until it is thoroughly fixed in my mind. The next day I repeat what I have made to a copyist. To work out my hymns I must be alone and quiet. Many have asked me why I always carry this little book, and hold it in my hand while I am speaking. Well, that is just one of my habits and I never think of leaving home without it. Sometimes it is a copy of the Psalms, or the

New Testament, or a book of daily quotations. When reciting my poems, sometimes a word escapes me, but by raising this little book towards my face my memory is prompted and the lost word brought back. At this advanced age I can recite my long poems without difficulty and talk to large audiences for an hour without being tired out. There is nothing in this wide world that gives me so much joy as telling the story of my Saviour's loving mercy.

> This is my story, this is my song,
> Praising my Saviour all the day long;
> This is my story, this is my song,
> Praising my Saviour all the day long.

"My love for the Holy Bible and its sacred truth is stronger and more precious to me at ninety than at nineteen. I have no time to cavil over the sacred volume or raise questions of no value about the Word. I go to the Book to find God and man's relation to Him. There I see

The little book Fanny Crosby always held in her hand when speaking in public

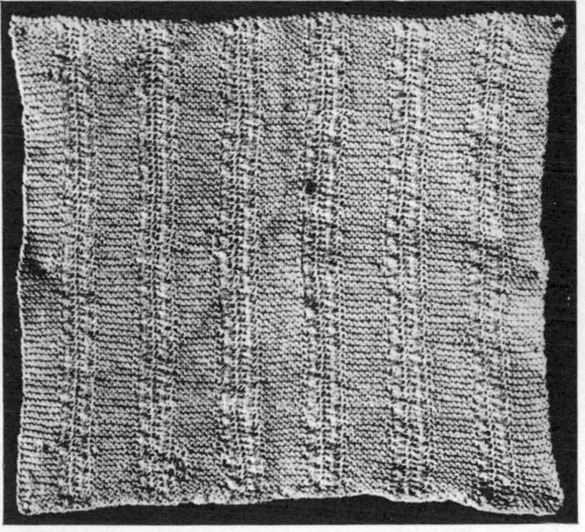

"Aunt Fanny's" industry: "She delighted in knitting wash-rags for her friends."

Christ as representing God's spirit in human flesh. This Book to me is God's treasure house and there is nothing I love better than to have my friends read to me from the sacred page. It is my bread of life, the anchor of my hope, my pillar of fire by night, my pillar of cloud by day. It is the lantern that lights my pathway to my Paradise Home.

"As I look down the avenue of these ninety years I find that I have been interested in everything that has been advanced for the welfare of the greatest number of mankind. Standing on the ninetieth golden step I look backward and see the pathway of struggle and victory. I take a glance forward, and lo, heaven's sunrise breaks in splendour on my brow.

Here let me wait with patience,
  Wait till the night is o'er;
Wait till I see the morning
  Break on the golden shore."

The service ended. Aunt Fanny shook hands with hundreds of people, then went with me to the manse. She took a cup of tea, and went to her room, there to sleep as peacefully as a little child.

XV

"Some Day, Till Then——"

Some day the silver cord will break,
And I no more as now shall sing:
But, O the joy when I shall wake
Within the palace of the King!

And I shall see Him face to face,
And tell the story—Saved by Grace.

Some day my earthly house will fall:
I cannot tell how soon 'twill be:
But this I know—My All in All
Has now a place in heaven for me.

Some day, when fades the golden sun
Beneath the rosy-tinted west,
My blessed Lord will say, "Well done!"
And I shall enter into rest.

Some day,—till then I'll watch and wait,
My lamp all trimmed and burning bright,
That when my Saviour opes the gate,
My soul to Him may wing its flight.

[*1891*]

XV

"SOME DAY, TILL THEN——"

"Some day,—till then I'll watch and wait,
My lamp all trimmed and burning bright,
That when my Saviour opes the gate,
My soul to Him may wing its flight."

ON Friday morning, the twelfth of February, 1915, the news flashed around the globe that Fanny Crosby, the world famed hymn-writer, had quietly passed into the Better Land. On Thursday night she was about, as usual. At nine o'clock she dictated a letter and poem of comfort to a bereaved friend, whose daughter had been called to the House of Many Mansions.

Here is the letter:

"*Thursday Evening.*

"*My dear, dear friends :*

"What shall I say? How shall I comfort you in this hour of your bereavement? I can scarcely realize that the white-robed angel has entered your home and left you desolate; yet no, you are not desolate, for there comes a message of inspiration that whispers to you all: 'What I do ye know not now, but you shall know hereafter.' And you know that your precious Ruth is 'Safe in the arms of Jesus.'

> You will reach the river brink,
> Some sweet day, bye and bye;
> You will find your broken link,
> Some sweet day, bye and bye.
> O the loved ones waiting there
> By the tree of life so fair,
> Till you come their joy to share
> Some sweet day, bye and bye."

She retired to rest and nothing was heard until about three in the morning, when Mrs. Booth, with whom she resided, thought she heard footsteps in her room. She quickly went to Fanny, took her in her arms, when the sightless singer became unconscious. Two physicians were immediately called, one of whom said, "Why, Fanny's been dead ten minutes."

"Oh, it cannot be," said Mrs. Booth. They sought to restore her to life but without avail. Her spirit had fled.

Letters of condolence poured in from far and near. On the day of the funeral many who had been associated with Aunt Fanny in life stood by her silent form as she lay in her casket. She was always fond of flowers, and her favourite blooms were everywhere apparent. She seemed to be sleeping in a bed of violets. A fact not usually known was that whenever she travelled she took along with her a little silk American flag. As she lay asleep that silk flag rested in her right hand, and was buried with her.

George C. Stebbins, with whom I sat at the funeral service, said to me, "Fanny wrote for the hearts of the people, and she wrote even better than she knew. She imbued all she ever did with a befitting spirit—the spirit of sweetness."

Ira Allan Sankey, Hubert P. Main

George C. Stebbins, and S. Trevena Jackson were the honourary pall-bearers. Long before the services began the church was filled to its utmost capacity. Ministers of all the churches from the city and surrounding country, together with many from other cities, attended. Representatives of church and patriotic organizations were present in large numbers. It was said to be the largest funeral service ever conducted in the city of Bridgeport.

The floral decorations were in keeping with the beauty of the dead singer's life. Four tall palms were arrayed along the pulpit platform. The first was decorated with white roses and white carnations. Between the first and second palms floral pieces were arranged. The second palm was arrayed with red tulips and white lilies. In the centre of the platform was a bower of flowers, consisting of a plaque of frezias and Roman hyacinths, a spray of narcissus and violets. In this bower of flowers lay a cross of narcissus. The third palm was trimmed with pink roses and Easter lilies. Between this and the last palm was a wreath of frezias, violets, and magnolias. Then a heart of white carnations and narcissus. The fourth palm was decorated with white roses and Easter lilies and near it a bunch of violets and wheat, sent by Aunt Fanny's old hack driver.

The choir, with the congregation, sang Aunt Fanny's favourite hymn, "Faith of Our Fathers." The Rev. H. A. Davenport, of the People's Presbyterian Church, led in prayer. The choir sang, "Safe in the Arms of Jesus" and "Some Day the Silver Cord will Break." Rev. Geo. M. Brown, pastor of the First Methodist Episcopal Church, of which Fanny Crosby was a member, said in part: "You have come to pay tribute, and to crown a friend. There must have been a royal welcome when this queen of sacred song burst the bonds of death and passed into the glories of heaven. She had been anticipating the time of her coronation. Of late she talked more freely of this hour than she had been accustomed to. Her later writings are full of it, as witness the following entitled 'A Little While':

'A little while to sow in tears and meekness,
The precious seed along the vernal plain,
Till into life the tender blades expanding
Fresh promise gives to summer's ripening grain.

'A little while we weep for those we cherish,
As one by one they near the river's brink,—
A little while to catch their sweet assurance
That we in heaven shall find each broken link.

'A little while! and thus the glorious dawning,
Of that fair morn beyond the swelling tide,—
When we shall wake, and in our Saviour's likeness,
Perfect and pure we shall be satisfied.'

"My text for this occasion is taken

from Second Timothy 4:1—'I have fought a good fight, I have finished my course, I have kept the faith, henceforth there is laid up for me a crown of righteousness, which the Lord, the righteous judge, shall give at that day.'

"Like myself I am sure you feel that words are inadequate to tell the story of Fanny Crosby's greatness and goodness.

"By her faith, her hope and her love she more nearly exemplified the Christian graces than any other person I have ever known. Her faith was rich and full, with no taint of doubt to lessen the sweetness of her assurance. If she believed too much she lost nothing by it in this life, and certainly not in the life into which she has entered.

"In the thousands of hymns she has given to the world a false note is not sounded. Faith, hope and love—these three chords were always dominant. I doubt if she ever had a pessimistic thought, and she counted her blindness among her blessings. No discouraged mortals ever went to her for help but carried away a new song of hope in their hearts. Her great desire was to help the sinful to a better life, believing as she always did that

> 'Down in the human heart, crushed by the tempter,
> Feelings lie buried that grace can restore;
> Touched by a loving hand, wakened by kindness,
> Chords that were broken shall vibrate once more.'

"Her hymns have won thousands to penitential tears. And it is not to be wondered at, for she believed that no man sank so low but that he could be reclaimed by salvation."

Dr. Brown went on to say it would be a most fitting thing for Bridgeport to build their proposed new Rescue Hall in memory of Fanny Crosby, to be known as the Crosby Memorial. She was pre-eminently their poet, their guardian angel, their hope. The speaker dwelt on the assistance that Fanny Crosby has been to those who had once lost hope in Divine favour, but who now had been brought back into the light of pardon. A Crosby Memorial would be an honour to the city and would always be a distinguishing mark. Dr. Brown closed his address by reciting a poem sent to him by Eliza Edmunds Hewitt of Philadelphia, author of "Will There Be Any Stars in My Crown," and other hymns:

"Away to the country of sunshine and song,
Our song-bird has taken her flight;
And she who had sung in the darkness so long
Now sings in the beautiful light;
The harp-strings here broken are sweetly re-
strung
To ring in a chorus sublime;
The hymns that on earth she so trustfully sung
Keep tune with eternity's chime!

"What heart can conceive of the rapture she knows
Awakened to glories so bright,
Where radiant splendour unceasingly glows,
Where cometh no shadows of night!
Her 'life-work is ended,' and over the tide,
'Redeemed' in His presence to stand,
She knows her Redeemer, for her crucified,
'By the print of the nails in His hand.'

"O 'Blessed Assurance'—the lamp in her soul
That made earthly midnight as naught!
A 'New song' of joy shall unceasingly roll
To Him who her ransom had bought.
To 'Rescue the Perishing,' her great delight,
What bliss, in the Homeland, to meet
With those she had told of the Lord's saving might,
Together, to bow at His feet.

"Good-bye, dearest Fanny, good-bye for a while;
You walk in the shadows no more;
Around you, the sunbeams of glory will smile;
The Lamb is the Light of that Shore!
Some day we will meet in the City above;
Together, we'll look on His face;
Safe, 'Safe in the Arms' of the Jesus we love;
Together we'll sing, 'Saved by Grace.'"

Printed in the United States of America